Fractions, Percentages, Decimals and Proportions

FRACTIONS, PERCENTAGES, DECIMALS AND PROPORTIONS

A LEARNING-TEACHING TRAJECTORY FOR GRADE 4, 5 AND 6

Frans van Galen
Els Feijs
Nisa Figueiredo
Koeno Gravemeijer
Els van Herpen
Ronald Keijzer

TAL-project
Freudenthal Institute for Science and
Mathematics Education, Utrecht University

SENSE PUBLISHERS
ROTTERDAM / TAIPEI

A C.I.P. record for this book is available from the Library of Congress.

ISBN 978-90-8790-572-9 (paperback)

Published by: Sense Publishers,
P.O. Box 21858, 3001 AW Rotterdam, The Netherlands
http://www.sensepublishers.com
Printed on acid-free paper

Translated into English by: Charles Frink
Editorial support: Liesbeth Walther, Meryem Tatar, Betty Heijman, Nathalie
Kuijpers, Nick Spier

Pictures Frans van Galen

This book was originally published in Dutch in 2005 as:
Breuken, Procenten, Kommagetallen en Verhoudingen;
Tussendoelen Annex Leerlijnen Bovenbouw Basisschool

Contents

Foreword

The book "Fractions, Percentages, Decimals and Proportions" is the third publication in the series "Learning-Teaching Trajectories for Primary School Mathematics", known by the Dutch abbreviation TAL. The themes of previous TAL-publications are whole numbers for grades K-6 and measuring and geometry for grades K-2.

The TAL-project was initiated by the Dutch Ministry of Education, Culture and Science. The aim of this project is to contribute to improving the quality of mathematics education by providing a global overview of educational goals and teaching-learning trajectories, and the relationships between them.

The structure of this book differs in a number of ways from previous publications. This has to do with the fact that the topics - fractions, percentages, decimals and ratios - are some of the most difficult parts of the primary school curriculum. A great deal of school time is spent on these parts of the curriculum, and the benefits are often disappointing.

In practice, this leads to a choice for streaming classes into groups of different levels, slowing the rate at which new material is introduced and lowering the didactic goals. An underlying problem, however, is the alignment of the curriculum. This concerns a great deal of subject matter that must be divided between a limited number of school years, with the consequence that pressure to teach more quickly is felt from the beginning. As a result, the development of a good, insightful foundation is liable to be pushed aside - especially for the students with weak mathematics skills. We have therefore chosen to shift the emphasis from "acquired skill" to "understanding". Our philosophy is that investing in core insights leads to better results.

Of course, space for this approach must be created. However, this does not have to result in a limitation of the attainment targets for all students. By investing in core insights, a foundation is established that can be built upon - in ways that differ between the students. During this process, we have chosen for differentiation as part of teaching that involves structural interaction with the children as an entire - heterogeneous - group; we believe this aspect is so important that we have devoted a separate chapter to it. The aim of differentiation within interactive education is ultimately to ensure that as many students as possible achieve the highest possible level. The education must then be structured in such a way that all students are given the opportunity to develop themselves further. To this end, we believe it is important for situations to be created that challenge students to think about more difficult questions.

Various considerations have led to a different structure than the previous TAL publications. The description of the learning-teaching trajectory is more global and the accent lies on a description of the didactical core. Moreover, we have chosen for an integrated description of the attainment targets in a separate chapter, instead of including the final and intermediate targets in the running text. This was done for two reasons. First, in this book we want to emphasize the coherence between the various parts of the curriculum, and second, because this concerns a relatively brief period at the end of primary school, which makes an extensive separation into interim goals less useful.

The publication of this book was preceded by a process of experimentation and discussion. The experiments took place at a number of experimental schools, where specially designed lessons functioned as a catalyst for discussions with teachers from the upper grades of primary school.
The broader discussion with teachers, teacher educators, school counsellors and other parties involved was conducted based on presentations and publications - including a tentative elaboration of the most important choices in the form of a discussion memorandum.
In addition, a website was opened with lesson descriptions, lesson experiences and explanations. The many reactions we received in various settings have led to important improvements. We would therefore like to thank all those involved for their contribution. We would like to give a special word of thanks to the teachers at the experimental schools.
Finally, we would like to express our appreciation of the staff of the SLO (Netherlands Institute for Curriculum Development) who made important contributions from a parallel project.

We hope that this description of the field of fractions, percentages, decimals and proportions not only provides a handhold and a global overview, but also is a source of inspiration for teachers, students, teaching instructors, supervisors and other actors in education. It is only through them that this book can provide its intended contribution to the improvement of the quality of mathematics education.

TAL-Team
Utrecht, May 2008

1 Introduction and overview

Emphasis on insight

The field of fractions, percentages, decimals and proportions is a complex and difficult one. The programme for grades 4, 5 and 6 appears to be overloaded, and the objectives appear to be attainable for only some of the students. Are the objectives for mathematics education set too high? A look at the core objectives established by the Ministry of Education of the Netherlands does not seem to confirm this. With respect to fractions, percentages, decimals and proportions, the objectives are formulated as follows:

> The students learn to understand the principal features of quantities, whole numbers, decimals, fractions, percentages and proportions and to make computations with them in practical situations.[1]

However, the concrete objectives are set down in the mathematics methods and the tests used at a specific school, and it is at this level that the teachers have ascertained that the programme is unfeasible for many students. As a solution, some schools have chosen to work with "level groups" that go through the material at their own rate. The risk of this approach is that some students never get to certain topics in grades 5 and 6, and at the end of primary school they may have hardly worked with percentages and decimals at all. In view of the importance of percentages and decimals in daily life, but also in view of the expectations of secondary education, this is an undesirable situation.

This book argues in favour of a different solution: to shift the emphasis from "acquired skill" to "understanding". Or perhaps it would be better to shift it even further, because the implementation of the methods in modern mathematics textbooks already puts a great deal of pressure on insight and understanding. Nevertheless, there are still high demands placed on skill levels, as if we assume that all students will ultimately master the subject matter in terms of a relatively formal system of rules and procedures. We must acknowledge that a large percentage of the students can learn to work insightfully with fractions, percentages, decimals and proportions, but only at a concrete level – within meaningful contexts and with familiar numbers.

If we focus on teaching arithmetical procedures instead of on developing insight, the emphasis comes to lie on individual exercises. The pressure that is felt – "you must get through the book" – ensures that teachers take too little time for class conversations and discussions. However, it is exactly these conversations and discussions – and not the lists of sums – that ensure in-depth understanding for the students.

This book essentially calls for the following shift: that students should not be required to achieve such a high skill level. On the other hand, it calls for higher demands to be placed on their reasoning capacity. In concrete terms, therefore, this leads to a change in the way time is spent in teaching, because more emphasis is placed on class conversations and discussions and less on individual practice. However, we want to emphasize that this concerns a relative shift; in addition to understanding, skill remains important.

This shift in emphasis also means that we want to link the objectives and interim objectives of the curriculum to "core insights", and not to the mastery of procedures. We will return to this aspect later.

Proportions

Proportion as a comprehensive concept

The comprehensive concept in the "fractions, percentages, decimals and proportions" curriculum is that of proportion. In a certain sense, fractions, percentages and decimals also describe proportions. Fractions indicate the proportion between a part and a whole. Percentages indicate the proportion of a specific total that is set to 100. Decimals are often measuring numbers that indicate the proportion with respect to a specific measurement.

When we refer to "proportions" in this book, we will sometimes refer to proportion as a comprehensive concept and sometimes to the typical grade 3 through 6 curriculum material concerning proportions. With the latter we mean – somewhat roughly formulated – the type of exercise where the ratio table plays an important role. In Chapter 3, we will focus primarily on this part of the curriculum from grades 3 through 6: reasoning with proportions. Essentially, we will place proportions next to the fractions (Chapter 4), percentages (Chapter 5) and decimals (Chapter 6), as part of the total curriculum. In Chapters 1 and 2, in which we will sketch out the coherence of the curriculum, we will use proportions primarily as a comprehensive concept.

Measurement numbers or proportion numbers

At a very early age, children observe proportions and can also describe them, although initially in qualitative terms. This is shown in the following example.

> Alexli, six years old, is sitting in the backseat of the car and looking at the ships on the river. One of them has an automobile on its deck. "Now, that is a big boat", she says. She indicates the size with her hands, first holding them close together and then very far apart: "if the car was this big, then the boat is this big!"

Cars are big for a child of six, but the boat is a great deal bigger. Alexli uses her hands to show the relationship between the size of the car and the boat. In a sense, she makes an image of this proportion.

Later on, students learn to describe proportions in quantitative terms, but not immediately in the form of "this much compared to this much". Often, proportions are captured in a single number, such as "five times as big", "two times as small", or "three times as expensive". In many cases, the proportions are hidden at an even deeper level, in what Freudenthal refers to as "measuring or proportion numbers". Numbers, he argues, appear in many forms to the students. In this context he distinguishes various aspects of numerical understanding.[2] For example, we can make a distinction according to:

- Labelling numbers. When numbers are used as a label, as with the numbers of bus lines, "Line 14".
- Ordering numbers. When it concerns the sequence of the numbers in a counting row, and adding forwards and backwards within the row.

- Counting numbers. This refers to the cardinal aspect; a quantity as an indicator for a set of countable objects.
- Measuring numbers. This is the number aspect that, according to Freudenthal, occurs most often in practice. In practical situations, we are frequently concerned with questions such as "how big" or "how expensive"; to answer these questions, standard measurements or other references are used to put matters into perspective.
- Calculation numbers. We can directly associate this number aspect with teaching; it concerns working with numbers that are separated from practical contexts. This concerns rules, properties and relationships between numbers. In this context we also refer to unlabelled numbers.

When measuring, you look at "how often something fits". For example if the meter stick fits seven times into a specific length, then we refer to a length of seven meters. This seven meters in fact indicates a proportion, the proportion between the length of a single meter and the total measured length. This is why measuring numbers can also be referred to as proportion numbers. Proportion numbers can be explicitly linked to a standard measurement, but we can also refer to other units, such as "half of the population", or "three-fourths of a bar". The "half" and the "three-fourths" in these examples are also proportion numbers; in fact, in practical situations, fractions are almost always proportion numbers. In summary, it is no wonder that Freudenthal came to the conclusion that most of the numbers we use in daily life are measuring numbers or proportion numbers.

Relationships and differences

The fact that fractions, percentages and decimals are so closely related makes it possible, when doing arithmetic in everyday situations, to move from one form to another and then back again. A few examples:

- With 75%, we think of three-fourths, with 73% we think of "almost three-fourths".
- 59% is "59 of 100" or "nearly 6 of 10"
- We recognize "20 of 60" as "exactly $\frac{1}{3}$".
- We interpret € 2.50 as $2\frac{1}{2}$ euros.
- We calculate three times € 2.50 by multiplying $3 \times 2\frac{1}{2}$, and we then interpret $7\frac{1}{2}$ as € 7.50.

The transition from one form to the other helps us to understand situations better and often makes the arithmetic easier. Fractions take a central role in this process. It is essential that students learn to see how fractions, percentages, decimals and proportions are related to each other. This is the backbone for the insight that they must develop.

Besides the relationships between these forms, it is also important that students understand the differences. If we can move so easily from one form to another, why do we continue to use fractions, percentages, decimals and proportions? Is this only an inheritance from the past, or are the differences still important? In Chapter 2, we will show how these fractions, percentages, decimals and proportions came about and how they apply to various types of situations and problems. Stated in an elegant fashion, they have a different phenomenological basis. It is important that students learn to acknowledge the differences and to see the value of these differences.

Students must therefore not only understand the relationships between fractions, percentages, decimals and proportions and be able to use these relationships, but they must also know why in one situation you use one descriptive form and in a different situation another descriptive form.

Labelled and unlabelled

First context-linked

Learning arithmetic begins with reasoning in concrete, practical situations. Working with numbers is initially linked entirely to a specific context. Later on, numbers can be separated from such situations and can begin to form a world of its own in the thinking of a child.

We can explain this by making an excursion into early arithmetic. At a certain point, very young children cannot answer the question "how much is four plus four?", even though they can combine four blocks with an additional four blocks and refer to this as "eight". For these children, "four" does not yet have independent meaning. For them, numbers exist only as labelled numbers: four blocks, four marbles or four ice creams. For that matter perhaps it would be better to refer to "adjective" numbers, because the numbers are used as a kind of adjective to typify quantities.

Later on, the children realize that "four plus four" is always "eight", regardless of what the numbers refer to. In time, a child learns more and more relationships between numbers, and these numbers consequently acquire a more abstract meaning. At that point, a child, when reading the word "four", no longer thinks initially about quantities, but about number relationships linked to the concept of "four", such as $2 + 2 = 4$; $3 + 1 = 4$; $5 - 1 = 4$, $2 \times 2 = 4$ and $8 : 2 = 4$. At this point, numbers no longer have a direct relationship with blocks or other concrete objects; they have essentially become objects themselves.

With fractions, percentages, decimals and proportions, a similar process must take place. We will explain this using fractions. These are initially labelled numbers as well, in the sense that students know what three-fourths of a pizza is, or three-fourths of a chocolate bar or of a line. Here as well, they must make the transition from labelled numbers to independent, unlabelled numbers. This means that "three-fourths" becomes embedded in number relationships such as "$\frac{3}{4} = \frac{1}{2} + \frac{1}{4}$; $\frac{3}{4} = 1 - \frac{1}{4}$", etc. However, this transition is only useful after students have been able to sufficiently explore the meaning of fractions. Unfortunately, teachers do not always take enough time for this exploration; the transition is then made before the students are actually ready and before they have been able to establish a network of relationships between fractions themselves. Often, concrete illustrations – such as fraction circles – are then used to fill in this gap. However, this turns matters upside down. Instead of students discovering the relationships between fractions by means of reasoning and generalization, they simply copy the relationships from an idealized model.

The language that teachers and students use here can lead to misunderstandings. A teacher who says "one-fourth and one-fourth together is one-half", may be referring to the relationship between independent, unlabelled fractions, while students can only see a relationship between concrete objects. For them, "one-fourth and one-fourth together is one-half" is the same as "two quarter circles from the fraction box together are the same size as the half circle." With respect to fractions, these students are still at the level of labelled numbers. This miscommunication is not obvious in the conversation between the teacher and the student because both appear to be speaking the same language.

Building a network of relationships

Ultimately, students must also develop knowledge that is separate from concrete situations. In other words, they must make the step to fractions as unlabelled numbers. We will refer to the knowledge that they develop over time about the relationships between various types of fractions as a network of relationships.

Students at the end of grade 4 probably know a reasonable amount about simple fractions such as "one-half", "one-third" and "one-fourth". During grades 5 and 6, their knowledge about fraction facts continues to grow. Students develop a network of relationships based on reasoning and doing arithmetic in context situations, therefore from situations with labelled fractions. While doing so, students will develop a network of relationships with which they can solve simple fraction problems. Regarding the tasks that we give to them, it is a good idea to begin with simple cases – as in early arithmetic. If the students are not presented with too many different fraction relationships, there is a greater probability that they will include these relationships in the network of relationships. Gradually, the network of relationships can be expanded. The rate at which this occurs will differ between students. However, at a certain point a limit will be reached, because they cannot have ready knowledge about all relationships between all possible fractions. At a certain point the students must make the transition to procedures, as they did when learning the whole numbers.

We must acknowledge that some students cannot make this transition. They are able to solve problems with simple fractions, but they do this based on the specific relationships that they know, and not based on general arithmetic procedures. Although we do not believe it is essential for all students to make this transition, they should still be given the opportunity to think about general procedures for adding, subtracting, multiplying and dividing fractions. Situations that can lead to the development of procedures should be regularly presented to the students. For students who didn't catch on to the procedures the first few times, this gives them another opportunity. But for the other students as well, it is not enough for them to reinvent or understand things only once. Even the better students must often come to understand the same thing several times before it sticks.

The distinction made above between unlabelled and labelled numbers applies not only to fractions, but also to proportions, decimals and percentages. The development from "labelled" to "unlabelled" applies to all numbers; it is essentially the same process as described in the TAL-publication

"Children learn mathematics", using the trio "context-bound counting-and-calculating", "object-bound counting-and-calculating" and "pure counting-and-calculating".

Models

In the learning process, models play an important role. Initially, models are very close to context situations. A pastry bar that must be divided can be illustrated as a drawn bar, or a strip of paper that must be folded; this is the context. During the initial period, students sometimes take their drawing literally; if two bars of one-fourth together are coincidentally longer than a single bar of one-half, then they conclude that one-fourth plus one-fourth is more than one-half. However, drawing a bar, number line, circle or other object should support reasoning, not confuse things.

After a time, students can also reason based on models outside a concrete context situation. For example, they can reason that $\frac{3}{5}$ is more than $\frac{1}{2}$ because $\frac{3}{5}$ divides a bar into one large piece and one small piece. Models gradually develop into independent aids for reasoning about fractions, percentages, decimals and proportions. However, the link with concrete situations remains very important. For example, students must still be able to imagine a concrete sharing situation behind the abstract division of the bar.

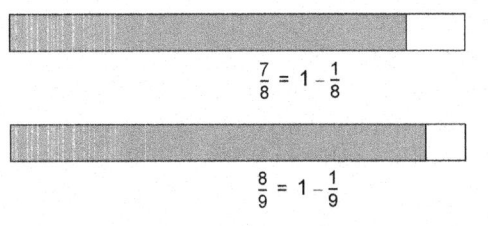

$$\frac{7}{8} = 1 - \frac{1}{8}$$

$$\frac{8}{9} = 1 - \frac{1}{9}$$

There is a difference between using models as we discuss them here and working with ready-to-use models such as fraction sticks and wooden fraction circles. In itself, working with such concrete materials is not wrong, but there is a risk that *reading off* relationships will take the place of *reasoning* about relationships.

For example, with such ready-to-use models students could "read off" that $\frac{8}{9}$ is larger than $\frac{7}{8}$, but not determine this by reasoning. The reasoning with these fractions could be, for example, that both fractions are nearly 1, but that $\frac{1}{9}$ is smaller than $\frac{1}{8}$, so $\frac{8}{9}$ is closer to 1.

In global terms, we can say that models are developed from models of concrete situations into models for reasoning. Simultaneously, a network of number relationships develops – which is supported by the models. After such a network of relationships has been established, the models can be used at another level. In this book we emphasize the use of the double bar and the double number line. This does not mean that other models shouldn't be used, but there are advantages to focusing on these two models.

Due to the double scales, these models provide a very clear picture of the relationship of the corresponding units. An example is the percentage bar shown on the right. The top scale indicates the numbers – for example the numbers of interviewees – and the bottom scale indicates the percentages. We will address models in greater detail in Chapter 2.

Guided reinvention

If we want to provide students with insight, we must also address fundamental questions about the functions of fractions, percentages, decimals and proportions. Examples of such questions are the following:

- Why do we also use percentages in addition to fractions?
- What is the advantage of using decimals instead of fractions?
- What do proportions and fractions have to do with each other?
- What do proportions and percentages have to do with each other?

These are the types of questions that build the foundation for a true understanding of fractions, percentages, decimals and proportions. Instead of asking the questions afterwards, when the students are already familiar with the topics, we believe it is better to use them as a point of departure for the introduction of these types of numbers. Essentially, we allow children to reinvent decimals and percentages themselves.

We refer to this process as "guided reinvention". Mathematics was invented bit by bit; mankind spent thousands of years in this process. This partly concerns concepts that are now so self-evident that we do not even realize that they had to be invented. For example, take the concept of zero. We need the zero in order to make a distinction between numbers such as 103 and 13. Nevertheless, the zero was invented in India only around 600 AD. At that time, the Romans continued to use separate symbols – *C* and *X* – to make a distinction between 100 and 10. In itself, this is also a clear system, but calculations with Roman numerals are much more difficult than with our "Arabic" numerals.

In a comparable fashion, the step from fractions to decimals was a tremendous invention. It was not the invention of a single individual, but the Dutchman Simon Stevin (1548-1620) was one of those who saw the advantages of decimal fractions and contributed a great deal to their acceptance.

The concept of guided reinvention is derived from Freudenthal.[3] He believed that we should give shape to education in such a way that we give the students the opportunity to essentially reinvent the discoveries of our forefathers. Of course, we should not take this too literally, because we cannot expect normal primary school students to do something that mankind took centuries to accomplish. However, under the guidance of the teacher, students can go through a process in which they discover for themselves that decimals are useful and why they are useful. Because the teacher plays an essential, guiding role, we refer to this process as *guided* reinvention.

Core insights

In this book, we advocate a shift in education from "acquiring skill" to "understanding". In later chapters, we will try to describe exactly what it is that students must understand, and in that context we will refer to "core insights". Here we want to explain what we mean by core insights. As an example, we will use the following problem.

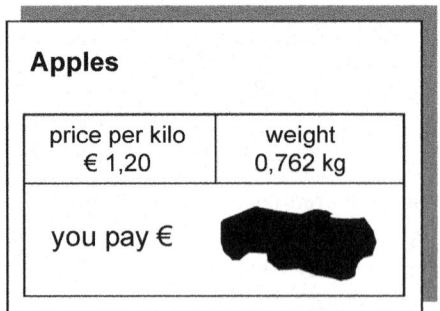

The price sticker on a sack of apples shows the total weight of the apples and their price per kilo. However, there is a blob of the ink on the total price. Approximately how much should you have to pay?

Students who see that this is a multiplication problem, $0.762 \times €\ 1.20$, can determine the solution directly, and with a calculator they have the answer right away. But for students from grades 5 and 6, it is not at all self-evident that this concerns a multiplication problem. Quite the contrary, when we presented this exercise to students, it turned out that they had no idea how they could solve this problem with a calculator. We will return to this in Chapter 6.

We formulated the exercise in a very open fashion: "*Approximately* how much should you have to pay for the apples?" Due to this open formulation, and with the concrete context as a support, almost all the students came up with sensible answers such as:

– 0.762 kg is less than 1 kg, therefore you would have to pay less than € 1.20.
– If one kilo costs € 1.20, then 100 grams cost € 0.12. Therefore the apples would cost slightly more than 7 × € 0.12.
– – 0.762 kg is approximately $\frac{3}{4}$ kg, therefore the apples cost about 3/4 of € 1.20.

We can use these answers to give an idea of what we understand by the term "core insights". If we ask the students to explain their solutions, it turns out that a great deal of insight has been involved.

– The first answer is based on the reasoning that the price of a sack of apples will be less than € 1.20, because it contains less than 1 kg. But how do you see that a decimal number is less than one? Of course, a rule can be used here, but really understanding how this works requires essential insight into the structure of decimals.
– Realizing that less than a kilo of apples costs less than € 1.20 requires insight into proportions. Based on a price of € 1.20 per kilo, you can not only calculate the price of 2 kg or $\frac{1}{2}$ kilo, but also of $2\frac{1}{2}$ kilos.
– For converting 0.762 kg into weight in grams, insight into changing measurement scales is required. To support this process, we can ask the students to imagine a double bar or a double number line, with grams on one side and kilograms on the other.
– Realizing that 0.762 kg is approximately $\frac{3}{4}$ kg requires not only that students link 0.75 to $\frac{3}{4}$, but also that they must see the relationship between 0.762 and 0.75. This has to do with insight into the order of magnitude of decimals. A feeling for numbers plays an important role

here. In this way, the students can also understand that 762 grams is very close to 750 grams, and is therefore approximately $\frac{3}{4}$ kilo.

The above example concerns the following: insight into the structure of decimals, into proportions, into changing measurement scales and into the order of magnitude of decimals. These are all matters that touch on the core of the actual understanding of decimals and proportions. An example of something that does not belong to this core would be doing arithmetic with decimals. This arithmetic – a procedure where the decimal divider is "moved" or "put back" later on – is no more difficult than doing arithmetic with regular numbers, but without the necessary insight it is simply a trick with a big chance of error. By focusing on core insights, we believe that imparting insight must have priority, and not teaching arithmetic rules. Knowledge of arithmetic rules is vulnerable if it is not based on understanding. Stated another way, students who do not know the arithmetic rules that are needed in a specific situation can still go a long way with their understanding of fractions and proportions.

In Chapters 3 through 7, we will describe the core insights and the corresponding didactical consequences in more detail.

Differentiation

The problem of the differentiation between students is often more severe when fractions, percentages, decimals and proportions are being taught than is the case with other subject matter or during other school years. In a certain sense, the programme for the upper grades of primary school is overloaded; there are many topics to be discussed and it is unfeasible to expect that all students can master the subject matter at a relatively formal and abstract level. Differentiation in speed, where some of the students proceed through the arithmetic book more slowly, is not a good solution. One consequence of this approach can be that students at the end of primary school have practiced endlessly with adding fractions, while they know hardly anything about percentages or decimals. In that case, the priorities have been incorrectly chosen, because adding fractions is not an important skill in daily life, while we encounter percentages and decimals everywhere we go.

The feeling of an overloaded curriculum especially has to do with the demands that we impose with respect to formal reasoning. There are enormous differences between students in this regard. When a new topic such as decimals or percentages is introduced, there are students who understand the system almost immediately and can reason with it at an abstract level; but there are also students who don't get any further in primary school than working with decimals or percentages in very concrete situations. To a certain extent, we have to accept such differences, and this means that the objectives in mathematics education must be modified. The basic principle must be that every student in primary school should develop an elementary understanding of subjects such as fractions, percentages, decimals and proportions, but at the same time we must accept that a number of students will only learn to calculate with such numbers in concrete situations. However, we must stimulate them as much as possible to also understand the system at a more formal level.

Modifying the objectives of the education involving fractions, percentages, decimals and proportions means that we must carefully consider the sums that we have the students practice, because these often assume that the students can reason at an abstract level. Take addition of fractions as an example. We will first look at adding fractions from the viewpoint of the students who are good in arithmetic. You can then say that "$\frac{1}{2} + \frac{1}{3} = \frac{5}{6}$" is just as real for the better students as adding "$65 + 17 = 82$", where you also don't have to know whether this concerns apples or the length of boards. Such children can also deal with sums such as "$\frac{3}{4} + \frac{2}{5} = ?$", because the abstract calculation rules are sufficient for them. However, for some of the children, adding fractions will only have meaning if they have a concrete context. In a sharing situation with $\frac{1}{2}$ pizza and $\frac{1}{3}$ pizza, they can find a correct solution, but as an abstract sum, "$\frac{1}{2} + \frac{1}{3} = \frac{2}{5}$" is just as acceptable to them as "$\frac{1}{2} + \frac{1}{3} = \frac{5}{6}$".

If we have all the students complete all the exercises in the arithmetic book, then they will practice a great deal on solving abstract fraction problems. However, these abstract exercises and the corresponding arithmetical operations have little meaning for them; as a result, they make mistakes. The teacher then perhaps decides that they should practice even more with this type of sum, but this does not increase their understanding. At most, they become more skilled at what they experience as a "trick".

As a second example, we can take percentages. Some students will require no more than an initial introduction with percentages to understand the scope of the concept of a percentage. They immediately see that percentages are a special type of fraction – "hundredths" – and they can effortlessly convert percentages into fractions and the reverse. For other students, however, the link between fractions and percentages must be made much more emphatically. Without that understanding, abstract conversion sums are useless, because even "25% is one-fourth" can have the same status as the fact that "horse" is "cheval" in French.

During the last years of primary school, mathematics education often pushes too quickly through to formal arithmetic. This results in students practicing arithmetic rules without understanding the foundation of these rules. Such education is not very effective, because practicing rules does not increase the students' insight. We therefore choose to focus on the development of insight. This means that more time must be taken for class discussions, because insight develops primarily through discussions and conversations. In such discussions, the most important thing is not the exact answer; what is important is the reasoning on which children base their solution. The time that must be made available for this process can be found by placing less emphasis on practicing arithmetic procedures. We believe that mathematics education should focus on core insights and global calculation.

Overview

In the following chapters, we will continue to work out the themes that we have briefly discussed in this chapter. The examples that we will use originated from the core lessons that have been developed (see Foreword).
In Chapter 2, we will discuss why it is important that fractions, percentages, decimals and proportions are not taught as separate parts of the curriculum. Students must be given the opportunity to continually discover relationships between them.
In Chapters 3 through 6, we will describe the core insights. Despite the fact that we want to avoid the strict separation of these parts of the curriculum, for the purposes of clear organization we have divided the topics of the chapters into fractions, percentages, decimals and proportions.
In Chapter 7, we will address the problem of differentiation. Because class

discussions play such a central role in education, we will extensively address what it means to involve all the students – also the weaker students and the fast learners – in the class discussions.

Finally, in Chapter 8 we will provide a description of the objectives and interim objectives in this complex area of subject matter. We will do this in a final chapter and not during the descriptions of the core insights in Chapters 3 through 6, because many objectives concern the coherence within the specific part of the curriculum.

notes

1 Ministerie van OCenW (March 2004). *Voorstel herziene kerndoelen basisonderwijs.*

2 Freudenthal, H. (1973). *Mathematics as an Educational Task.* Dordrecht: Reidel.

3 Freudenthal, H. (1991). *Revisiting Mathematics Education, China Lectures.* Dordrecht: Kluwer Academic Publishers.

2 Relationships

Introduction

The relationships between fractions, percentages, decimals and proportions or ratios can be dealt with in a natural way if we make the context the central feature in teaching, and give students the chance to explore these contexts in many different ways.

Fractions, percentages, decimals and proportions are different descriptions of something we can, in a certain sense, consider the same. In the following situations it is the same proportion that is being considered:

- Wieke ate $\frac{3}{5}$ of her chocolate bar.
- 3 out of 5 car drivers are regularly in traffic jams.
- This food is made up of 60% water.
- It is still 0.6 km to the campsite.
- Three parts sand to two parts cement.
- The fraction $\frac{3}{5}$, with no context given.

This chapter covers the relationship between fractions, percentages, decimals and proportions. Fractions, percentages and decimals and proportions all have in common that they represent a ratio between what is being described and the unit it is being referred to. These similarities mean we can easily change between these forms in everyday situations, which helps us to interpret the situation and solve the problem. At the same time this relationship also helps us to better understand the numbers. The box on page 28 shows an example.

Context situations provide a constant reason for changing from one form to another. This fact can be used for teaching that is based on everyday situations. The relationships between fractions, percentages, decimals and proportions can thus be dealt with in a natural manner.

We will begin this chapter with a historical-mathematical reflection by describing how fractions, percentages and decimals arose.

Uncertainty on vote result

More than 60% in favour of adapting zoning plan

No two-third majority for plan

12 out of 19 councillors

The relationship between fractions, percentages, decimals and proportions is evident from the fact that we can often change from one form to another. Mostly we make that transition without noticing it. Consider the following situation:

> The town council has just taken a vote. 12 of the 19 councillors voted to change the zoning plan, but there is still uncertainty about whether a two-thirds majority is required. The local newspaper reporter wonders how she can put the voting proportions in the headline for her article.

A description with "12 out of 19" – a proportion – says too little for a headline. In any case, more than half of the councillors were in favour. Half of 19 is $9\frac{1}{2}$, so 10 councillors is already a majority.

But according to some councillors, a two-thirds majority is required; was this reached? It is easiest to work from 12. The 12 voting for the motion would be two-thirds if the council had 18 members. But the council has more members – 19 – so the two-thirds majority was not obtained.

How many percent is 12 of 19? If an estimation is good enough, we can do it without a calculator. 12 of 20 would be 6 of 10 and thus 60 of 100. So 12 of 19 would be slightly more than 60%. To work out exactly how many councillors were for the motion, it's easiest to use a calculator. 1% of 19 is 0.19. We must divide 12 by 0.19, leading to a rounded off result: 63%.
On the calculator we can also work it out by 12 : 19 = 0.6315789. You could say this is changing the fraction $\frac{12}{19}$ into a decimal number. We can translate this into $\frac{12}{19} = \frac{63}{100}$, which agrees with 63%.

After this we will move on to the teaching and describe which models are important. These models support the acquisition of knowledge about number relationships, amongst other things.

And finally we will show how fractions, percentages, decimals and proportions can be addressed together if we give "rich" mathematical problems – problems which students can approach in many ways – a more central place in teaching.

Different but still the same

The history of how fractions, percentages, decimals and proportions arose shows that different situations require a different manner of notation.

Why are there different ways of writing the same proportion? History offers an explanation. Each new notation arose to fit a specific situation or a certain manner of calculating. The differences between situations still play a role today.

Proportions

Fractions, percentages and decimals represent proportions. We speak of proportions if there is a linear relationship between two (or more) numerical descriptions. "Linear" or "directly proportional" means: if one number is increased or decreased by a certain factor, then the other number is also increased or decreased by that same factor. Such a relation occurs frequently, for example:

—   Price and weight. If you buy twice as much, you usually pay twice as much.
—   Fuel consumption. If a car does "32 for 1" it means that you can drive 32 kilometres on 1 litre of fuel and therefore 64 kilometres can be driven on two litres, or 48 kilometres on one and a half litres.
—   Ingredients. To keep the same flavour for a dish, the amounts must be increased or decreased in direct proportion.
—   A scale model, of a car or a plane for example. All the dimensions must be reduced proportionally.

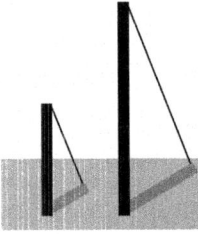

– Shadow. There is a linear relation between the length of vertical sticks and their shadows. A stick that is twice as tall has a shadow that is twice as long.

A difference between descriptions of proportions such as "2 out of 3"or "32 to 1" on the one hand, and fractions, percentages and decimals on the other is that in the first case the two numbers in the proportion are both named, whereas for fractions, percentages and decimals the proportions are essentially summarized in one number. So $\frac{7}{25}$ metre means that this length and the length of one metre are in the proportion $\frac{7}{25}$: 1. In the same way 0.28 m means that the measured length and one metre are in the proportion $\frac{28}{100}$: 1. That is also an important reason why these notations arose: people wanted a concise way of stating the proportional situation.

Fractions

Fractions, percentages, decimals and proportions are initially described by action language. You divide, you round off or you construct a new measure by dividing by ten or a hundred. From this, numbers and number relationships can be developed, but we can see from the history of fractions that this was not such a simple process.

When the Egyptians developed fractions around 1700 BC, they only used unit fractions - fractions with 1 as the numerator. The picture shows how $\frac{1}{7}$ was written. The Egyptian notation was used well into the Middle Ages. In cases where a simple unit fraction was not directly available, people resorted to adding a series of unit fractions.

We can ask why fractions with numerators other than 1 were not introduced in earlier times. One possible explanation is that unit fractions first have to be seen as countable objects before you can introduce "numerators" as a useful concept.

If you work a lot with a certain unit fraction, the action aspect will fade into the background and the unit fraction gains the status of an independent measure. Consider, for example, $\frac{1}{4}$ litre of cream. For us that is a specific amount for which we no longer think of dividing a litre into four parts. The action aspect has completely disappeared, but we are still aware of the proportion: one litre is four times as much as $\frac{1}{4}$ litre. Once a new measure has taken form we can start measuring with it. Only then is it meaningful to expand the language of fractions and to introduce fractions with numerators not equal to 1, because these new fractions then describe the number of times something can be measured off. This explains why the transition to using numerators larger than 1 was not automatic. It is not just about extending a procedure from "dividing" to "dividing and multiplying". There is a step in between: the "one-so much-part" must first acquire the character of an independent measure.

Percentages

Percentages arose from calculating with money. Initially, interest and taxes were expressed as a proportion. Interest could be given as: for every 300 ducats, 5 ducats interest will be paid. At the introduction of a new Dutch tax system in 1569, it was stated that every "tenth coin" had to be paid as tax, so one in every ten coins.

Working with such proportional numbers has a disadvantage in that comparing proportions is difficult. Is two out of three more or less than three out of five, for example? To solve this problem people started working with a standardized proportion by calculating with "out of one hundred". The French "per cent" was adopted and stands for a proportion in which one of the numbers is set to 100.

Decimal numbers

It was only around 1600 that people had the idea of decimal fractions. The Dutch author Simon Stevin explained the system in a book entitled De Thiende (The Tenth). The advantage of decimal fractions or decimals – Stevin did not use a decimal point for writing them at that time – is that you can use them in arithmetic as if they were normal numbers. Moreover, you can refine them endlessly in a simple manner: if 3.6 is not accurate enough you can use 3.64 or 3.642, etc. It is an elegant system that incorporates the decimal structure of the whole numbers – units, tens, hundreds, etc. – to the right of the decimal point.

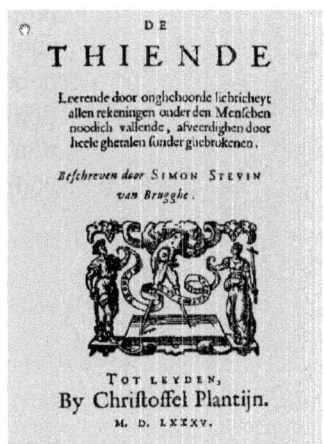

With the arrival of typewriters, calculators and computers, the use of decimals has really taken off, and now we use decimals in many situations in which fractions were previously used.

One difference between decimals and percentages is that percentages always stand alone, as it were, whereas with decimals you can work just as easily as with whole numbers. You can add a decimal to another number or subtract it.

Standardization

Percentages and decimals are easier to compare than fractions and ratios.

–   In descriptions such as "$\frac{1}{3}$" and "$\frac{2}{5}$" you cannot see immediately which fraction is larger. If you change the fractions into decimals, it then becomes obvious: 0.333… and 0.4.
–   To determine which mix or proportion contains the most juice, it is easier to compare 33% "pure fruit juice" and 40% "pure fruit juice" than "1 part juice to 3 parts water" and "2 parts juice to 5 parts water".
–   No one needs to think about the question of which is larger, 33% or 40% of some amount of money. Percentages are standardized to one hundred, which makes them easy to compare, and we can see immediately by how much two percentages differ.

At a certain point in time people decided to standardize fractions and proportions to avoid problems when making comparisons. Fractions led to decimals via standardizing the refining in steps of ten. Percentages arose from the standardization of proportions to one hundred.

Insight into the relationships between fractions, percentages, decimals and proportions leads to making an easy change from one descriptive form to another. This relationship is shown in the figure. The term "proportional notation" is given between quotation marks because it also applies to fractions, percentages, decimals and proportions. We use "proportional notation" to mean a description such as "2 out of 3", i.e. descriptions in which both numbers of the proportion are stated separately.

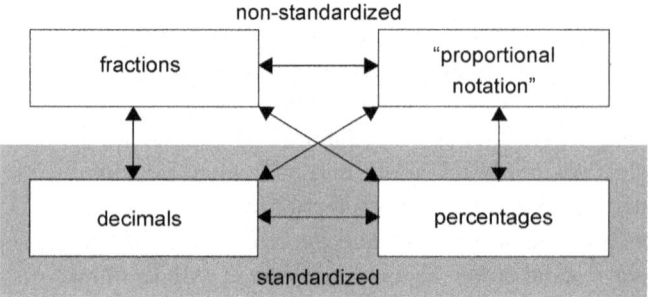

A few examples:

- If we want to calculate 9% of something, we can do that by entering *0.09 on the calculator (from percentage to decimal).
- Working out the sum "$\frac{1}{2} + \frac{4}{5}$" becomes easy if we change to decimals. We then add "0.5 + 0.8 = 1.3" (from fractions to decimals).
- If 75% is indicated, we need to take $\frac{3}{4}$ (from percentage to fraction).
- To work out "0.49 + 0.249" we make an estimate and calculate "$\frac{1}{2} + \frac{1}{4} = \frac{3}{4}$" (from decimals to fractions).
- 3 out of 5 people is 60% (from proportion to percentage).
- "$\frac{2}{3}$ of 75 people" is "2 out of 3 people", or "10 out of 15, or "50 out of 75" (from fractions to proportions).

The examples clearly show that it is sometimes easier to change to a standardized description of a situation (in percentages or decimals), but not always. The examples also show the great similarity between notation in decimals and in percentages (the standardized numbers): 0.75 and 75% are very close.

Didactical perspective

The history of how fractions, percentages and decimals arose offers pointers for how to structure their teaching.

We began this chapter by discussing the historical origin of fractions, percentages and decimals. A long development over time ultimately led to the use of fractions, percentages, decimals and proportions as we know them today. It seems logical to allow students the time to go through this development themselves, but in an adapted way. This will give them the opportunity to discover the relationships between fractions, percentages and decimals and to start to understand why percentages are chosen sometimes and fractions at other times. This process of gradual discovery can be guided by providing the students with suitable situations. We must guard against making the jump to fractions, percentages and decimals as independent, "unlabeled" numbers too quickly. The students should first be encouraged to build up their own network of relationships.

If we look at fractions, percentages, decimals and proportions from a teaching perspective, then it is clear that we should start with the characteristics of each type. If we want to discuss percentages, we should place the students in situations in which it is obvious to think in terms of "out of 100". If we want to make the step from fractions to decimals, we should encourage the students to see the advantages of working in a standardized form. Because we envisage learning as the active construction of a network of relationships, every approach should also quickly lead to investigating the relationships.

This relationship is emphasized again when fractions and percentages are visualized on a bar, or when whole numbers, decimals and fractions are located on the same double number line. These models will help students develop a language for fractions, percentages, decimals and proportions; since these models can essentially be shared by the various parts of the curriculum, a common language can develop. However, this does place demands on the teacher, who must be able to explain the relationships explicitly.

Making the relationships between fractions, percentages, decimals and proportions visible also puts demands on how the subject matter is built up, since this is where the origins of the concepts must be explored. Eventually the pocket calculator can also be a means of allowing students to think about the relationships between fractions, percentages, decimals and proportions.

Contexts and models

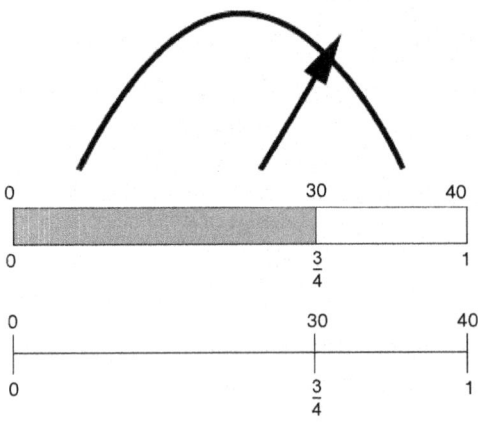

Fractions, percentages and decimals are proportional numbers which often gain meaning only when it becomes clear what they are applied to. For fractions, for example, a fuel gauge can be used.

The tank is about $\frac{3}{4}$ full. How far can you drive? That depends partly on how big the tank is. If it holds 40 litres, then you now have 30 litres; if it takes 60 litres, you now have 45 litres. The bar and the double number line make the relationships between litres and fractions explicit.

Within a specific context it becomes increasingly clear what a fraction, decimal or percentage refers to, and the situation will help students to choose the correct operations. At a higher level, models can fulfil this function. Well-chosen contexts enable students to make the transition to working with a bar or another model. In the context of a story about a baker, the students can be asked how they can divide a French loaf into six parts. It is natural to envisage the French loaf as a bar. Working from this sort of situation,

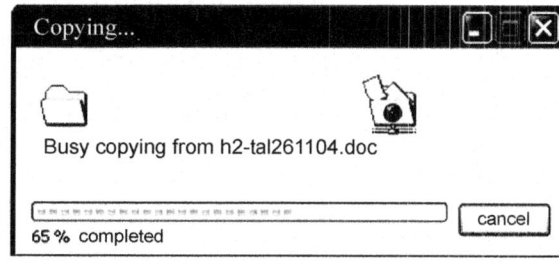

the bar can become a model for the students to imagine the procedure for dividing something into equal parts. The bar is the unit and at the same time the object to be divided.

Students will recognize the bar as showing the part that has already been downloaded or copied. The figure on this page shows that about two-thirds – 65% according to the computer – of the file has been copied. In this book we will mainly pay attention to the bar model and the double number line. However, these are not the only models that can play a role in this part of the curriculum. In some contexts, a rectangle or circle might be more suitable, and some fractions can be more easily read from these shapes. For percentages and decimals in general, the bar or the number line are the most obvious representational form to choose. They have the advantage that they can be used to express the proportional aspect of fractions, percentages and decimals by writing different numbers above and below the line. Moreover, these models are useful not only for representing concrete situations, but also for providing visual support when reasoning with number relationships. By using bars and number lines with fractions, percentages and, decimals – as well with as proportions – we make a clear connection between the different parts of the curriculum.

Towards a model for numerical reasoning

An important reason for focusing on the bar as a model is the opportunity it offers to explore number relationships. This takes place immediately during discussions with students over useful ways to divide a bar into six, eight or nine parts, for example. A bar can be divided into six by first imagining it being divided into two or three parts. Dividing it into eight parts can be done by mentally dividing it repeatedly into halves.

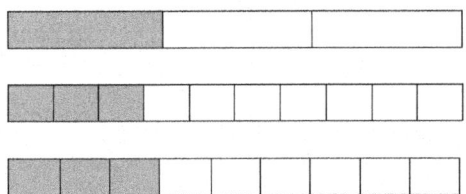

For comparing fractions – for example $\frac{1}{3}$ and $\frac{3}{10}$ – thinking of a bar also offers support. The $\frac{1}{3}$ fraction can be made by dividing the bar into three – drawn or as a mental image. For $\frac{3}{10}$ you can divide the bar first into two halves and then each half into five pieces. Finally, you take three of these pieces. The two bars that are made for this exercise can be laid on top of each other. But the process of making the divisions can also lead to reasoning. By dividing the bar first into three parts and then further, you can reach nine pieces and $\frac{1}{3}$ can also be seen to be $\frac{3}{9}$. When you realize that $\frac{1}{9} > \frac{1}{10}$, then you can reason that $\frac{3}{9}$ is larger than $\frac{3}{10}$.

The bar thus supports the formation of a network of relationships – in this example the relationships between $\frac{1}{3}$, $\frac{3}{9}$ and $\frac{3}{10}$. The function of the model changes with the step from context-linked fractions to fractions as independent objects. The bar becomes a way of showing how you have reasoned numerically.

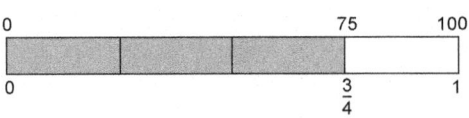

Numerical reasoning with bars reinforces the understanding of the relationships between fractions, percentages and decimals. We can imagine, for example, $\frac{3}{4}$ by thinking of a bar with four parts, in which we make a division between three parts on one side and one part on the other side. If we then want to see how many hundredths this signifies, we imagine the bar as four parts of 25 cm, or 25%, and take three of these parts. The bar shows how we can calculate this. It reveals that $\frac{3}{4}$ is the same as $\frac{75}{100}$ or 0.75. Moreover, the bar in this way shows the equality of the two proportions, namely 75 : 100 and 3 : 4. It also makes clear that $\frac{3}{4}$ is the same as 75%.

The bar is now no longer an abstraction of a context, but a means of organizing your thinking that is based on number relationships. The bar or double number line thereby eases the transition from fractions and proportions to decimals and percentages.

The double number line can be used, for example, in the earlier problem about the price of 0.762 kg of apples at € 1.20 per kg (see Chapter 1).

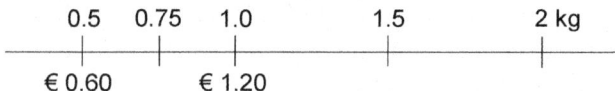

The price of 0.75 kg can be found by taking the average of the prices for 0.5 kg and 1.0 kg, or by halving the price for 1.5 kg. The double number line can be used in a similar way for reasoning about percentages.

Network of relationships

One aim of learning about fractions, percentages, decimals and proportions is that students develop a network of relationships. Such a network is the basis for reasoning about these subjects. We believe that the teaching should be aimed at encouraging students to acquire enough numerical relationships so that reasoning – often via estimations or global calculations – becomes possible.

In our view, a network of relationships is acquired primarily through estimation and global calculation. Working on this network of relationships helps the students increase their feeling for numbers. For nearly all students, 25 is a special number because it immediately invokes relationships with other numbers. This should also be the case with more numbers. For example:

– 49, which is nearly 50 and therefore half of 100
– 33, which is a little less than $\frac{1}{3}$ of 100
– 16, which can be repeatedly divided by 2
– 16, which is a little less than $\frac{1}{6}$ of 100
– etc.

Tackling a rich problem

Rich mathematical problems enable students to experience the relationships between fractions, percentages, decimals and proportions. A lesson on fuel tanks can illustrate this:

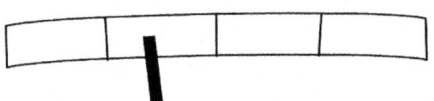

Gasoline
high octane lead-free
€ 1.299 per liter

The students are given a worksheet with the two pictures above, but no more than that. Sam says immediately that the left-hand picture is of a gasoline meter. Job: "It's a fuel tank." Johnny can explain how it works: if fuel is used, then the needle goes to the left. Sam tells why a fuel meter is important: otherwise you wouldn't know when your tank is nearly empty. The sign at the gas station is also discussed. Everyone agrees that you can round up € 1.299 to € 1.30. Eventually the students formulate their own problem: how much can you still put in the tank and how much will it cost?

The question about how much fuel will still fit in the tank can be answered estimating. Every part represents 15 litres; therefore no more than 20 litres is still in the tank, so you can add another 40 litres. The answer to the question on cost can also be estimated: 40 times $1\frac{1}{3}$, which is approximately € 52. If the teacher wants a more accurate answer to the first question, the students make finer divisions on the fuel gauge. Robert divides the parts of the bar into threes; Johnny does that too and tries to refine the bar even further to calculate the sums more precisely.

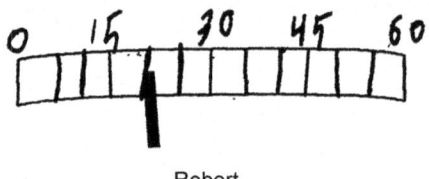

Robert

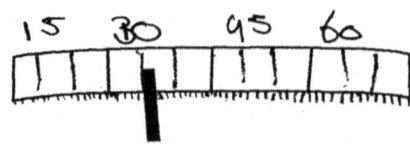

Johnny

During the discussion, it turns out that the best way to determine the total cost of the fuel is by making a ratio table. The students do this and all of them arrive at a cost of more than € 49.00.

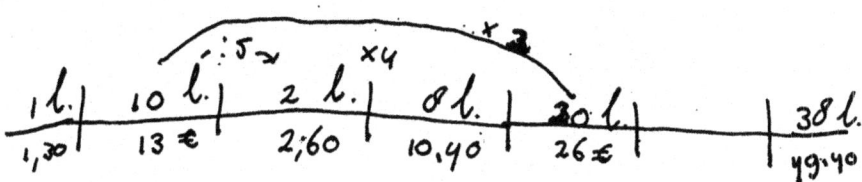

In the discussions that are elicited by the problem, the students make the step from proportions to fractions, from fractions to decimals, and so on. Such shifts in perspective have been made possible by the numerical relationships the students have in their repertoire. In this case, it concerns relationships such as:

–   Half of 60 is 30 and one-fourth is 15.
–   1.299 is approximately 1.30 or 1.3.
–   1.30 is approximately $1\frac{1}{3}$.
–   10 times 1.30 is 13 (or in more general terms: multiplying by 10 makes the ones into tens).
–   38 is comprised of 30 and 8, and 8 can be reached via 2.

We recommend that you explore what special numbers the students know and why they are special to them. If students can build a network of special numbers in this way, they will see that relationships from this network can be used in all sorts of ways.

–   You can get a 25% discount. If we recognize 25 as $\frac{1}{4}$ of 100, it is immediately clear that we need to pay $\frac{3}{4}$ of the original price.
–   What does 0.329 kg cost if 1 kg costs € 0.60?
    0.329 is approximately $\frac{1}{3}$, so the 60 must be divided by 3. It will cost about € 0.20.
–   How much is 30 : 2.37?
    We begin by measuring. 2.37 is approximately $2\frac{1}{2}$ and $4 \times 2\frac{1}{2} = 10$. Every time that we can measure off 10 from 30 stands for 4×2.37. Because 10 can be measured off 3 times from 30, the answer is approximately 12.

Relationships between fractions, percentages, decimals and proportions are also part of the network of relationships. These involve relationships between simple fractions and decimals such as $\frac{1}{4} = 0.25$ and their conversion into whole numbers and percentages: $4 \times 25 = 100$, $4 \times 2\frac{1}{2} = 10$, and $\frac{1}{4}$ is the same as 25%. Moreover, with a view to fractions and proportions, attention should also be paid to multiples of 12, because these can be divided by 2, 3, 4 and 6.

Summary

In this chapter we have called for a central place to be given to the relationships between fractions, percentages, decimals and proportions in mathematics teaching. History shows that there were good reasons for developing different methods of notation. If we want students to understand the relationships between these methods of notation, they essentially need to go through a similar development process themselves. A practical reason for paying attention to the relationships is that in many everyday situations it is useful to be able to change from one notation to another.
In the next chapter we will discuss the core insights that students need to develop. We will emphasize two models: the bar and the double number

line. These models are a means of representing number relationships and thus support the relationships between the forms of notation.

If we want students to really understand fractions, percentages, decimals and proportions, interaction with the students must be at the centre of the teaching method. Rich mathematics problems automatically elicit such interaction. An example of a complex problem is shown in the boxes on pages 38 and 39.

3 Core insights for proportion

Proportion in grades 4 through 6 involve reasoning and calculating with direct proportions. It is important that students recognize situations where proportions are being used. Calculating with proportions often has the aim of making situations comparable. In this respect they are closely related to fractions, percentages and decimals. In a certain sense, a proportion is a more general concept, which is reflected in fractions, percentages and decimals in a more specific way. The ratio table plays a large role in calculating with proportions. Students must not only be able to work with the ratio table when it is provided, but they must also be able to recognize situations where it can be useful.

Core insights

A quarter of the population can be stated as "$\frac{1}{4}$" or "25%", or given as a proportional description such as "1 in 4 people choose ...". A quarter litre can be written as "$\frac{1}{4}$ litre", "0.25 litre" or as "25 centilitre". There are many forms of mathematical descriptions with fractions, percentages, decimals and proportions, and they all have their own rules and procedures.

We can choose to teach students all these rules, but that often leads to them not being able to see the forest for the trees and mixing up the rules. Moreover, learning all these arithmetic rules requires a lot of practice, and experience shows that students quickly forget rules and procedures when the practice stops. This is particularly a problem in secondary school because the training is less intensive than it can be in grades 4-6. The programme for fractions, percentages, decimals and proportions - as stated here - appears to be too broad and complex for most students.

We propose here a simpler and narrower programme that does not aim at mastering procedures, but rather at understanding the underlying principles. The emphasis is shifted from skill - carrying out procedures - towards understanding. It is in this context that we refer to core insights; these are insights which make up the core of what students need to learn and understand.

Core insights indicate what the teaching should pay particular attention to. In the following chapters we will try to establish what the core insights should be for fractions, percentages, decimals and proportions, in that order. First, in this chapter, we will discuss proportion.

Proportions are everywhere

We encounter proportions everywhere:

— Enlarging and reducing: photos, copiers, models, maps, crazy mirrors.
— Money: price comparisons, get 4 for the price of 3, telephone rates, return tickets versus single tickets, exchange rates.
— Recipes for 4 or 6 people, making coffee.
— Comparing probabilities.
— Gears on a mountain bike, how steep the hill is.
— How shadows change during the course of the day, length of shadow with respect to size of object.
— Graphs and diagrams.

The list could be expanded much further. And mathematics lessons also involve proportions so frequently that "proportion" itself does not seem to have its own clear place in the curriculum.

Students already have a lot of experience with proportions by the time they reach the upper grades of primary school - although the assignments in these earlier years usually did not call them "proportions". In this book, which deals with grades 4-6 (children between 9-11 years old), we do not have the space to go into this earlier situation in detail, and we will limit our descriptions to teaching proportions in these grades. There are many size and measuring situations which involve proportions in earlier education, but these are dealt with in other books in the TAL series[1].

In Chapters 1 and 2 we discussed "proportion" as a mathematical feature in its broadest sense. We explained that fractions, percentages and decimals in fact also describe proportions, and in this sense "proportion" is a more general concept.

In this chapter we will pay attention to calculating with proportions and in this more specific sense, proportions can be placed next to and at the same level as fractions, percentages and decimals. They offer a certain descriptive manner - for example "2 in 5" - which in many cases can be changed into an alternative description using fractions, percentages or decimals.

We could say that in grades 4-6 we will concentrate on describing "direct" proportions, or on reasoning using proportions. For proportions in grades 4-6, the sums often involve searching for other number pairs to describe the same ratio as the given numbers. One of the standard aids to use for this is the ratio table.

In this chapter we will first discuss the concept of direct proportions. Then we go on to the ratio table, paying attention to the introduction of the ratio table and to the strategies that can be used when working with it. Then we move on to more problematic issues, such as composite units and absolute and relative comparisons.

Finally, we will return to proportions, but now to situations where there is a relationship between two units which is not directly proportional. In this book, when we refer to direct proportionality, we mean a linear relationship. We will close this chapter by sketching out a learning-teaching trajectory.

Reasoning with proportions

Proportions

We can state proportions in many ways:

- "The car gets 18 km per litre."
- "2 out of every 10 children are too fat."
- "You can go 18 km per hour if you cycle reasonably fast."
- "There are proportionally more girls in grade 5 than in grade 6."

Proportions are based on the concept of ratios (direct proportionality). "The car gets 18 km per litre", means that the number of litres of fuel that the car uses is directly proportional to the distance driven. We can deduce from this that driving 36 km requires 2 litres, 180 km requires 10 litres, etc. In a manner of speaking, the ratio "18 to 1" characterizes many number pairs.

A ratio table shows this clearly because we can expand the number of columns to suit our needs:

litres	1	2	10	11
km	18	36	180	198

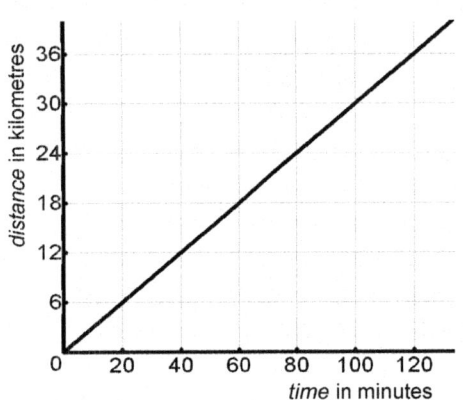

In mathematical terms, a directly proportional relationship between two units is called a "linear relationship". It is called this because it can be drawn as a straight line on a graph, and the line will pass through the origin if it is a direct proportion.

In the graph we can read off what happens if someone cycles at 18 km per hour. In 20 minutes he cycles 6 km, in 40 minutes he cycles 12 km, and in 90 minutes he cycles 27 km, etc. In zero minutes he cycles zero km, which is why the straight line goes through the origin, the point (0,0). The following ratio table represents this graph:

distance in km	9	18	36	54
time in minutes	30	60	120	180

Direct proportions occur frequently in everyday life, in fact we should say: in our thinking about everyday situations, since just because someone takes an hour to cycle 18 km does not mean that after 30 minutes he will be exactly halfway, or that he would cycle exactly 36 km in two hours. If we want to make predictions - How long will it take me to cycle to Arnhem? When will I need to refill the gasoline tank? - it is useful to be able to think in idealized relationships.

In reality, there is often only an approximately direct relationship. The graph and the ratio table above are not a description of a true cycle trip, but in fact a mental model.

The ratio table

The ratio table plays an important role in the curriculum on proportions in grades 4-6. It is an ideal aid for making handy calculations and gaining insight because the table invites students to write down intermediate steps. To calculate how long someone will take to cycle 20 km at an average speed of 15 km per hour can be done like this:

km	15	5	20
minutes	60	20	80

Not so long ago in grades 4-6, such ratio problems were often written down as "15 : 20 = 60 : ?" or "15 is to 20 as 60 is to …" This notation led to a manipulation of numbers that was not really understood by many students. In this respect, the ratio table is much clearer because every intermediate step has a meaning. In this case: "15 kilometres in 60 minutes means the same as 5 kilometres in 20 minutes". Moreover, the strength of the ratio table is that students can reason with number relationships which they already know. The table above could be from a student who has immediately seen that you can go from 15 to 20 with 5 as an intermediate step. Another student might choose to double the numbers as an intermediate step.

km	15	30	10	20
minutes	60	120	40	80

The ratio table can also be used for calculating with percentages and decimals. We will return to this subject briefly at the end of this chapter when we sketch out a learning-teaching trajectory. In Chapters 5 and 6 we will go into more detail on this aspect.

The ratio table is a mental model as well as a work sheet. The table helps students reason with proportions and is at the same time a handy calculation tool. It is important that students are continually aware of what their numbers signify.

Calculating in the ratio table

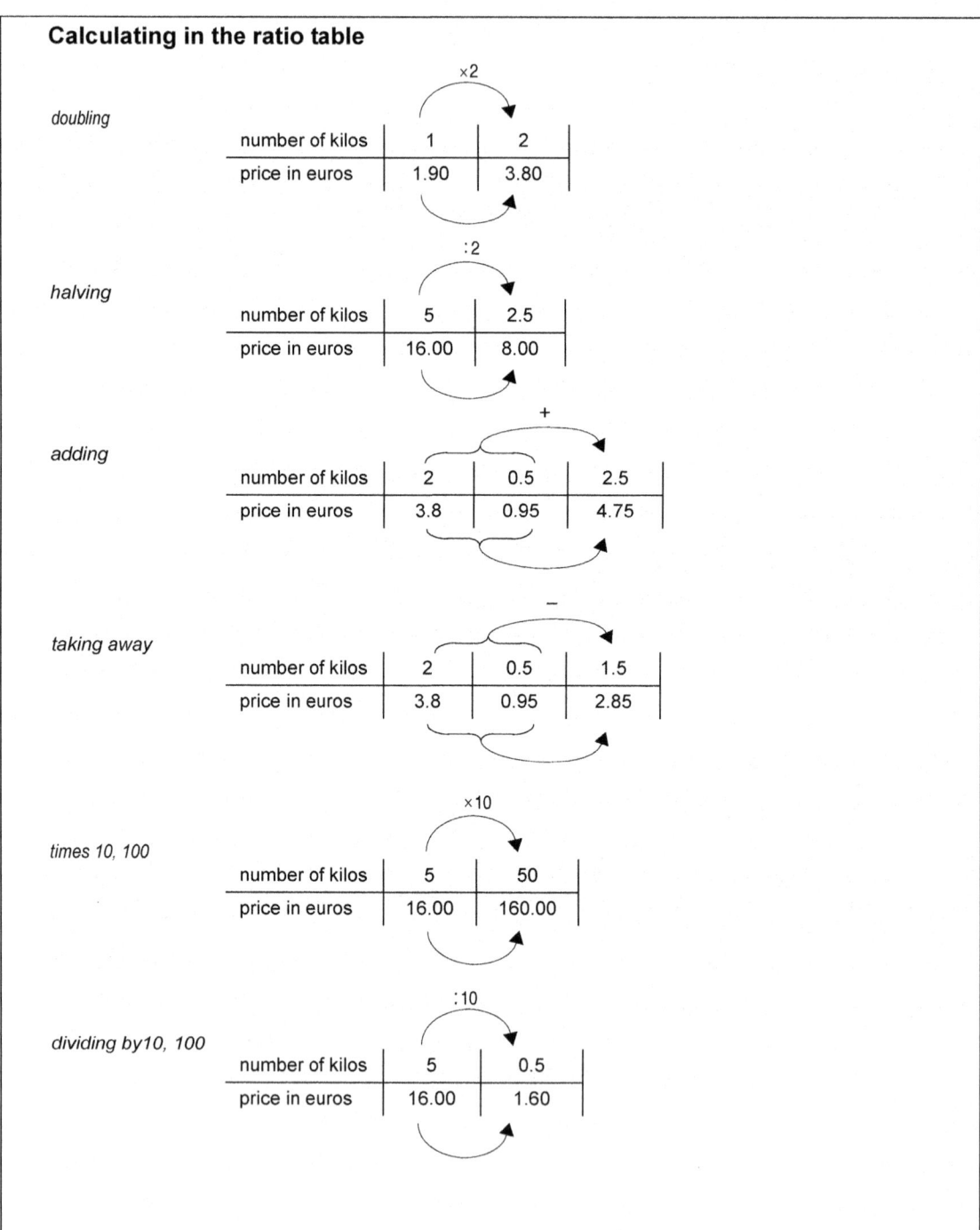

doubling

		×2
number of kilos	1	2
price in euros	1.90	3.80

halving

		:2
number of kilos	5	2.5
price in euros	16.00	8.00

adding

			+
number of kilos	2	0.5	2.5
price in euros	3.8	0.95	4.75

taking away

			–
number of kilos	2	0.5	1.5
price in euros	3.8	0.95	2.85

times 10, 100

		×10
number of kilos	5	50
price in euros	16.00	160.00

dividing by10, 100

		:10
number of kilos	5	0.5
price in euros	16.00	1.60

Within a context it is clear, for example, that you can multiply both weight and price by the same number, but that you cannot add the same number to both values.

weight	100 g	200 g	50 g	150 g
price	€ 2.00	€ 4.00	€ 1.00	€ 3.00

100 grams costs € 2.00

– You can double, because if you buy twice as much you have to pay twice as much. Therefore 200 grams costs € 4.00.
– You cannot add the same number to both: 150 grams does not cost € 2.50 (adding 50 to both the weight and the price).
– You can add columns to each other. If 100 grams costs € 2.00 and 50 grams therefore costs € 1.00, then 100 grams + 50 grams together cost € 3.00.

The box on page 48 gives examples of some steps that are possible in a ratio table. It is a good idea to discuss with students what can be done in a ratio table. That can be done best by referring to a context. And it is therefore important to always state the units being used. That can be done for each column, as above, or just for each row, as below.

weight (grams)	100	200	50	150
price (€)	2.00	4.00	1.00	3.00

As far as the notation goes, the ratio table gives a good overview, but is not in itself any better than a table or list in which the numbers are placed under each other. This is an example of a systematic list:

100 grams costs € 2.00
200 grams costs € 4.00
50 grams costs € 1.00
150 grams costs € 3.00

The advantage of the table is that all the numbers have their own place and that the unit of measurement must stay the same. In this respect, lists allow more freedom, but this is not always desirable.

Compare the above list with:

> 1 kilo costs € 20.00
> € 2.00 for 100 grams
> 25 grams for € 0.50
> You pay € 2.50 for 125 grams

Consequently, there are good reasons for choosing a ratio table as the standard form of notation, but that does not mean that the ratio table should be introduced - essentially imposed from above - without any discussion.

Reinventing the ratio table

To build students' understanding of the ratio table, it is good if they start working with the table from their own discoveries as much as possible. We must provide the students with the opportunity to reinvent the ratio table for themselves. In this respect, Freudenthal speaks of guided reinvention.[2] This "reinvention" should of course not be taken too literally. For example, it is not necessary for the children to have to think up the notational form of the table, since this notation is actually nothing more than an agreed standard. We showed in the previous section that a list with the numbers under each other could also be useful. The reinvention comes down to two things: the choice of a systematic notation method and discovering for themselves how useful a ratio table is for doing calculations.

Students first have to realize that a systematic notation method has great advantages. Children who use a worksheet often write down their intermediate steps in a rather chaotic manner. They will often write down a list of items more automatically than they will choose a table form, but by allowing them to compare lists, they can discover what they need to write down for the list to be complete. The transition from a systematic list - items under each other - to a ratio table with all the numbers next to each other is then not such a big step.

Then students need to independently explore which steps they can make in the table and which will not work. The overview on page 48 does not have to be learned by heart as a set of rules. Students can learn these rules by reasoning from a context problem and by explaining to other students how they have reasoned.

The teacher can help by making the mathematical steps in the table explicit.

A notation with arrows from one column to another can help clarify their reasoning. To do this, it is helpful if the children have developed the language and terms to describe what they have done. The boxes on pages 52 and 53 give an example of possible lessons on this subject.

Comparisons using proportions

In the supermarket we continually have to choose between two products, for example, jam with the supermarket's house brand or with a French brand. Which one costs less?

The French jam costs less, but it is a smaller pot. The supermarket pot is more expensive on the face of it, but "proportionally" the jam costs less. We can therefore consider the question about which pot costs less in two ways, *absolutely* and *relatively*. In the latter case, we make a proportional comparison. In the supermarket it is often easy to see a proportional comparison because the price per kilogram is given on the shelf label. If we have to calculate it ourselves, we can do this in several ways.

| 400 gram
€ 1,28 | 300 gram
€ 1,20 |

– We can calculate the weight of one in terms of the other, or vice versa. A pot of supermarket jam weighing 300 grams would cost:

weight (grams)	400	100	300
price (euro)	1.28	0.32	0.96

– Or the other way around: a pot of French jam of 400 grams would cost € 1.60.
– We could calculate the price for both jams for the same weight, as the supermarket does for us nowadays.
– It is handy in both cases to work out what 1200 grams would cost:

weight (grams)	400	1200
price (euro)	1.28	3.84

The ratio table as an aid for maintaining an overview

When do you need to use a ratio table and why is it useful? If we provide the ratio table together with the problem, then the students do not have to think about such questions. At times it is therefore good to present proportional problems as completely open questions. In the series of textbooks used by the school in this example, the ratio table has been in use since grade 3. Lia, a teacher in grade 5, wondered whether her students would use the ratio table spontaneously if it wasn't presented with the problem. She gave her class this assignment:

In the shop, cheese is priced at € 9.00 per kilo.
Each group must choose the weights of various pieces of cheese and work out how much each of the pieces would cost.

In the discussion the students proposed:

A quarter kilo costs € 2.25
One-third kilo costs € 3.00
One-eighth kilo costs € 1.12
750 grams costs € 6.75

The students did not use a ratio table on their work sheets. The teacher first discussed the relationship between a kilo, gram and a half kilo and then asked the groups to see whether the price for 750 grams in the list above was correct.

In the general class discussion, the students put forward various arguments. Then Fenne and Karlinde - who had proposed the piece weighing 750 grams - said that they had figured the price for 750 grams by first figuring the prices for 500 grams and 250 grams. The teacher wrote down everything the children said in a table, without commenting on it at that stage. Finally, on the blackboard there was the following table:

€ 9,00	€ 6,30	€ 0,45	€ 0,90	€ 6,75	€ 4,50	€ 2,25
1000 gr	700 gr	50 gr	100 gr	750 gr	500 gr	250 gr

The students understood the notation, but when the teacher asked what was the name for what she had written on the board, they said "diagram", "graph", "table", "gram table", "calculation table", "100 gram table" and "euro table".

The teacher explained the term "ratio table". In the following task - about cheeses that cost € 12.00 and € 15.00 per kilo, respectively - only some of the students went on to use a ratio table.

In several lessons after this, the teacher presented similar problems, including one on bags of candy with different weights. In each lesson she emphasized the importance of clear notation. Because the teacher always put her answers in a table, many of the students also used this notation, but there were also some students who preferred a vertical list of items. The teacher emphasized that they were free to do that, but only if their lists were neat and provided a good overview.

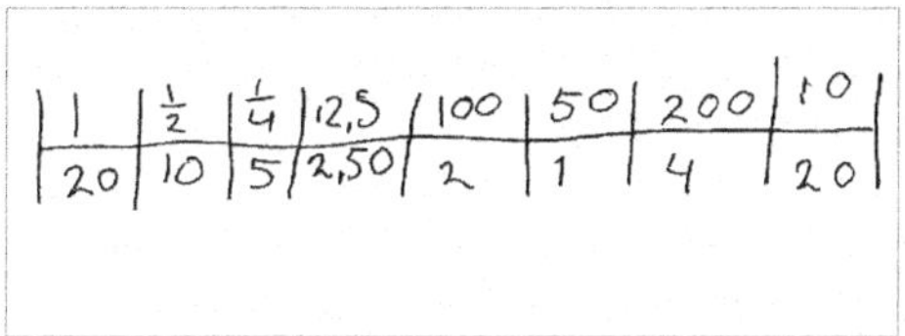

1	$\frac{1}{2}$	$\frac{1}{4}$	12,5	100	50	200	10
20	10	5	2,50	2	1	4	20

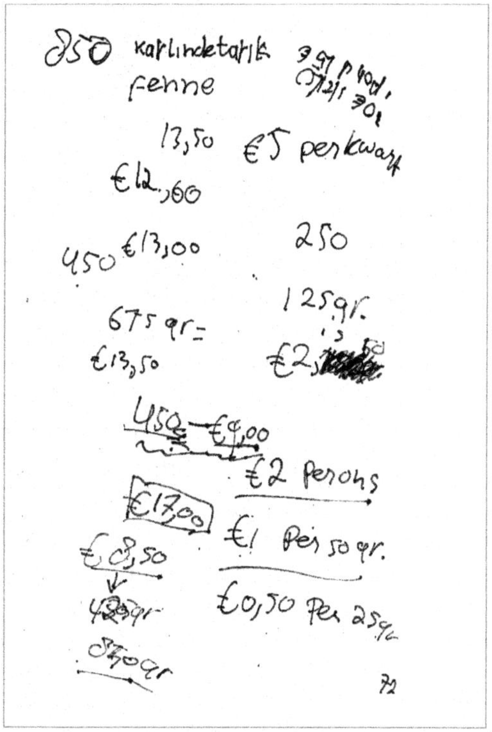

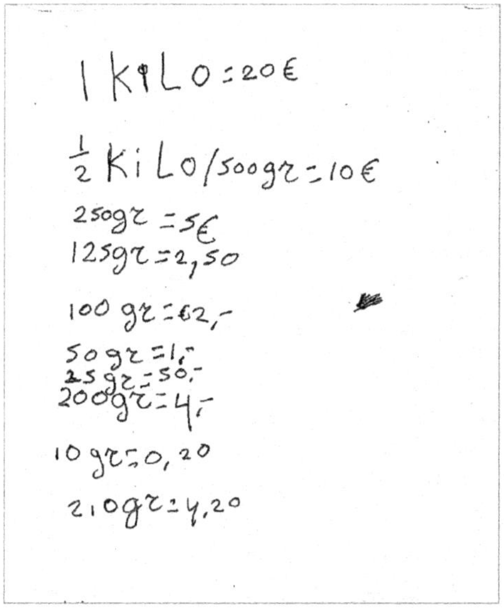

1 KiLO = 20€

$\frac{1}{2}$ KiLO / 500gr = 10 €

250gr = 5€
125gr = 2,50

100 gr = €2,-

50 gr = 1,-
25 gr = 50,-
200 gr = 4,-

10 gr = 0,20

210 gr = 4,20

850 karlindetariek 3 gr p kod,
      fenne   12, 30,

      13,50   €5 per kwart
    €12,60

450 €13,00   250

                125gr.
  675 gr =
  €13,50   €2,

  450 - €9,00
            €2 persons
     €17,00   €1 per 50 gr.
  €8,50
            €0,50 per 25gr.
  450 gr.

  850 gr.   72

The illustration shows the work by three groups on a task about candy for diabetics at € 20.00 per kilo. Fenne and Karlinde's worksheet - on the right - was very messy and the teacher commented on this. In later lessons the teacher often returned to make a point about clear overviews and notation, and the students were regularly given problems in which they had to choose their own form of notation.

weight (grams)	300	1200
price (euro)	1.20	4.80

– We could also, in principle, calculate to the same amount of money. With these numbers, that's easiest to do with a calculator. Then it becomes apparent that you get more supermarket house brand jam for the same amount, because you get 312.5 grams for € 1 compared to 250 grams of French jam.

Proportional comparisons are based on a mental experiment: suppose that there were 400 grams of jam in the pot, how much would that cost? Or suppose that we paid € 1.00, how much jam would we get? This latter step is rather artificial in this context, but just as correct for a mental experiment. In ratios between price and weight, the students have little trouble with the mental experiment underlying the conversion, because it is so logical to start from a directly proportional relationship between price and weight. In practice, smaller pots are indeed often more expensive "proportionally", but that is exactly what you can determine by recalculating. In other situations, many more presuppositions are required to be able to make a proportional comparison. For example, we can compare schools with different numbers of students regarding the number of students who stay for lunch at school or the number of children who cycle to school. We can then work as if the number of children at a school could increase accordingly. "Suppose the Johannes school has 400 students …" Another example is to compare the criminality in two towns by calculating the number of bicycles stolen "per 1000 residents". We are then working as if criminality is directly related to the number of residents in the town.

As adults, we are so used to thinking in proportions that we mostly do not realize that we are making an artificial mathematical transition. For children, the difference between absolute and relative comparisons is not nearly as self-evident. The box on page 56 describes an example of students who simply discarded some of the information in order to make the numbers the same.

The question is whether in teaching we focus sufficiently on the aspect of comparing absolute terms versus comparing in relative terms. What we mean is: do we present the students with enough situations in which they

have to make the transition to relative comparisons by themselves?
In other words, do we not give the students too many activities in which the method of comparison is pre-determined? If the ratio table is already shown on the worksheet with the two units indicated above and below the line, then the context problem becomes not much more than a calculation exercise.

Instead of emphasizing calculation exercises, we should encourage children to think a lot about the function of mathematical tools. This can be done via investigative activities and open questions without a pre-determined approach. Situations in which there appears to be a conflict between different information can especially encourage children to think. The emphasis in such activities should lie on the class conversations and discussions.

Composite units

Some situations refer to a proportion between one part and the total, for example:

—   3 out of 24 children in the class.
—   43 out of 150 Members of Parliament.
—   982 of the 1231 interviewed persons.

In such proportions we are only dealing with one "unit", the number of children, the number of members, the number of people interviewed. However, there are also situations in which we need to state the proportion numerically between different units:

—   Fuel consumption: number of kilometres per litre.
—   Velocity: km per hour.
—   Wages: euros per hour.

In such cases we speak of a composite unit. "Number of litres" or "number of kilometres" are different types of units and combining them leads to a new unit, namely "fuel consumption". In the history of mathematics it took a long time for such units to become accepted. For children composite units are also troublesome: velocity, for example, is a difficult concept. The ratio table simplifies calculations with composite units immensely because in such a table you can work with the separate units ("litres" and "kilome-

It should be just as many

Reasoning in terms of proportions is not as automatic as we sometimes like to think. The following example shows how students make the numbers comparable by simply ignoring some of the information provided.

The teacher explained the following problem to grade 5:

> The gym teacher is selecting players for the school basketball team. Julia, Tom and the other children have all had turns at trying to throw the ball through the basket as many times as possible. The black circles indicate the balls that scored and the white circles are the balls that missed. The eight children did not all throw an equal number of times. Can you still say who did best? Can you rank the players?

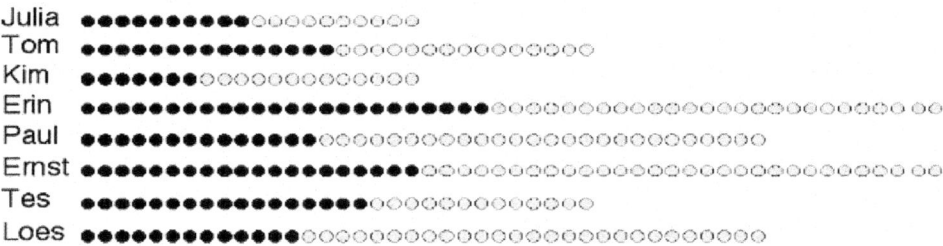

After the students discuss the questions in their groups for a few minutes, the teacher summarizes how far they had come. It appears that some of the groups had made the rows equally long by drawing a line through the circles after the first twenty, or had covered the ends of the longer rows with a piece of paper. They simply didn't count anything that was longer than the rows for Julia and Kim. The students think Erin and Ernst were the best because they only had black circles.

When this approach is discussed everyone eventually agrees that this is not a fair way of determining the best player. Two other types of reasoning are also proposed:

– There were groups who tried to convert the ratio of baskets-missed throws to another number. For example: if Kim had thrown 40 times she would have scored 14.
– Other students changed the proportions into fractions. Julia and Tom scored with half their throws, Kim scored with slightly less than half her throws, etc.

tres") rather than directly with the composite unit.

Composite units are special because in everyday life we often calculate with a standardized proportion. Fuel consumption is expressed in the number of kilometres you can drive on one litre of fuel: it is always "18 to 1" or "24 to 1" but never "90 to 5" for example. Velocity is given as the number of kilometres travelled in one hour, or - in other situations - the number of metres in one second. Price labels for products like peanut butter convert the price per pot to the price per kg to make it simpler to compare different brands. The advantage of such standardization is that we can make a direct comparison. The relationship between two numbers is essentially reduced to a single number. However, note that supermarkets are not always consistent because on the labels on the shelves they sometimes convert prices to 1000 grams, but the prices for vegetables and cheese are often for 500 grams and for a prime steak the price may given for 100 grams.

Supermarkets do this expressly because a price per kilo makes it very clear how expensive some items are.

How things are standardized is no more than a mutual agreement. An interesting illustration of the arbitrary nature of standardization is the following. In the Netherlands, vehicle fuel consumption is given as 1 litre for so many kilometres, and in the United Kingdom and the USA, they refer to the number of miles per gallon. However, Portugal uses a different system, where fuel consumption is expressed as the number of litres needed to drive 100 kilometres.

A mouse eats more than an elephant

An example of an indirectly proportional relationship is the fact that a mouse or bird must eat relatively more than an elephant. This is not just because small animals are more active than large ones, but also because they lose more heat. Animals lose heat via their skin - their external area - and small animals have a relatively larger external area. This can be illustrated with a simple set of blocks.

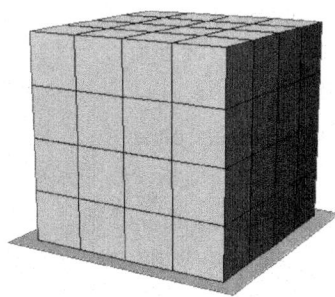

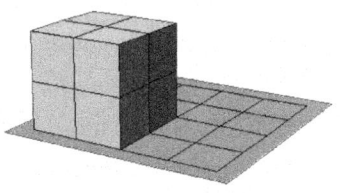

The building with 64 blocks has an external area of $6 \times 16 = 96$ squares. A building half as high and half as wide has a volume of 8 blocks and an external area of $6 \times 4 = 24$ squares. The volume of the second building is 8 times less, but its external area is only 4 times less. For a mouse and an elephant - which differ in size by much more - this difference in external area is even greater. A mouse loses a relatively large amount of heat and must compensate for this by eating more.

Indirect proportions

We speak of ratios or proportions if there is a direct relationship between units. Although directly proportional relationships are very common, we must still consider relationships that are not directly proportional. Consider mobile telephone rates. The cost of a mobile telephone call is usually made up of a starting rate and a charge related to the length of the call, so it already costs a few cents before the conversation can begin. In this situation, a four-minute call does not cost twice as much as a two-minute call.

Another example of an indirectly proportional relationship is that between length and area when enlarging a photo. If you enlarge a photo of 10 × 15 cm to 20 × 30 cm - the height of the photo is then twice as much - the area increases from 150 cm² to 600 cm² and is therefore four times larger. And if you make the height four times as much, the area becomes 16 times larger.

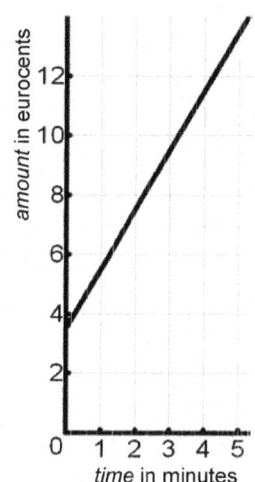

height	10 cm	20 cm	30 cm	40 cm
area	150 cm	600 cm	1350 cm	2400 cm

Children are often confused by the fact that making something twice as big does not make the area twice as big. This happens especially when the context does not offer much help. The relationship between length and area is not linear, but quadratic: the area increases by the square of the length. These examples also point to another important point: not every table is a ratio table.

The global learning-teaching trajectory for proportions

Before grade 3, students start with a broad exploration of proportions. This exploration primarily has a qualitative nature and covers situations dealing with dimensions and measuring. The students learn about simple visualization. Gradually, proportions are dealt with more quantitatively and, in this respect, we would like to point out the more hidden aspects of proportions in measuring numbers and ratios. We can distinguish several parts of this trajectory.

Ratio table

One of the parts of the trajectory involves the ratio table. After the ratio table has been carefully introduced, a feeling has to be developed for recognizing situations in which it can be useful. At the same time, strategies are developed for making clever use of the ratio table. Some students can then move on to more formal strategies, such as converting a given ratio into the required ratio using a standard method. For example, if the proportion "16 to 28" needs to be converted to "so many to 100", this can be done in just two steps via "dividing by 28" and "multiplying by 100".

	:28	×100	
16	0,5714	57	
28	1	100	

This strategy approaches the use of the multiplication factor, which is hidden in the table. The table can be seen as a multiplication table in which the bottom row is made by multiplying the numbers in the top row by $1\frac{3}{4}$. This is a formal approach which can be mastered by some students.

If we look at the contexts in which ratio tables are used, we can distinguish between situations where both numbers in the ratio refer to the same unit - for example when it involves part-whole relationships - and situations where the units differ and we are dealing with composite units. As we have said, composite units are more difficult to understand, but at the level of working with a ratio table this usually does not create any extra complications.

Percentages and decimals

Another part of the learning-teaching trajectory that lies very close to the above is using the ratio table for percentages and decimals. For percentages, this involves converting proportions to percentages as well as calculating with percentages.
Proportions or ratios can be converted into percentages by calculating "so many to 100". For example, this is a possible calculation for the question:

"150 of the 750 people interviewed agreed, what percentage is that?"

agreed	150	50	10	20
interviewed	750	250	50	100

The ratio table can also be easily used for calculating with percentages. For example, the question: "How many is 35% of 120?"

100%	25%	10%	35%
120	30	12	42

Or the question: "What percentage is 150 out of 750?"

100%	10%	20%
750	75	150

In calculations with decimals, the ratio table can be used especially for multiplication. The ratio table is an aid to multiplying with organized handy calculations and for changing the unit of measurement. For example: cheese costs € 6.40 per kilo. How much do you have to pay for 1.70 kilos?

1000 grams	500 grams	200 grams	1700 grams
640 cents	320 cents	128 cents	1088 cents

The ratio table is particularly well suited to global calculations and estimating the result using an iterative approach. Going a step further, the solution to division problems can be found by multiplying upwards.

Proportional comparisons

Another part of the learning-teaching trajectory concerns proportional comparisons. An important first step is to distinguish here between absolute and relative comparisons. The question "Which jam is cheaper?" can be answered by indicating the cheaper pot (absolute) or by choosing the jam which is cheaper according to the price-weight proportion (relative).

The next step is to extend into situations in which there is no strictly linear relationship, but where we act as if there is one. This concerns nearly all the situations where we use the expression "average … per …"; such as: "average income per head of the population", "average energy use per year", or "average number of goals per match". Such situations include average velocity, which is one of the reasons that velocity is such a difficult concept.

Indirect proportions

Finally, a subject that stands apart from the others is the attention needed for relationships that are not linear. To avoid misunderstandings on this point, attention must be paid to these relationships with a certain regularity.

notes

1 Heuvel-Panhuijzen, M. van den & K. Buys (red.) (2005). *Young Children Learn Measurement and Geometry.* A learning-teaching trajectory with intermediate attainment targets for the lower grades in primary school. Utrecht: Freudenthal Instituut.
TAL-team (2006). *Measurement and Geometry (provisional title). Learning-Teaching Trajectories for Primary School Mathematics.*

2 Freudenthal, H. (1973). *Mathematics as an Educational Task.* Dordrecht: Reidel.

4 Core insights into fractions

Fractions originate from situations involving division and measurement. In the contexts that they are used, they almost always have the characteristic of measurement or proportion numbers that refer to part-whole proportions. Historically, fractions were the first development in this area. They are the basis of understanding and reasoning with percentages, decimals and proportions. This requires understanding mutual relationships and the ability to use basic knowledge about fractions in a flexible fashion. Essentially, the students must be able to understand simple number relationships and conduct reasoned operations with fractions. An important aspect is being able to find common denominators and convert part/whole relationships into equivalent proportions.

Fractions as a foundation

Fractions in primary school

Should fractions still be taught in primary education? In daily life, common fractions (officially known as vulgar fractions) have been almost entirely replaced by decimals (officially known as decimal fractions) and percentages. Unlike fractions, you can use decimals on calculators, easily compare them with each other, and you can choose any desired level of accuracy by increasing or decreasing the number of digits to the right of the decimal point (officially known as the decimal divider). Percentages have the same advantages. Does this mean that fractions are only historically relevant? Shouldn't it be possible to start by teaching percentages and decimal numbers, and only bring up fractions when the situation calls for it, for example when you get to algebra?

We believe fractions still deserve an important place in primary education. There are two reasons for this. The first reason is that we often figure and think in terms of fractions, even when fractions are not explicitly involved. For example, if you have to estimate how much 72% of 600 is, you probably figure that 72% is about three-quarters. Then you figure that one-half of 600 is 300 and one-quarter of 600 is 150, so the answer is about 450.

Fractions give meaning to percentages and decimals, and they play an important role in mental arithmetic when percentages and decimals are involved.

The second reason is didactic in nature: if you understand fractions, you have a good foundation for proportions, decimal numbers and percentages. Modern mathematics teaching uses situations that children encounter in daily life and is based on the spontaneous approach children take to these daily problems. Many situations in daily life lead naturally to fractions, for example situations where we want to indicate how big something is compared to something else. When you draw a room, the following proportions apply: the door is twice as tall as the window, the closet is three times as tall as the stool. Viewed in terms of fractions, the window is half as tall as the door, the stool one-third as tall as the closet. If we want to estimate the number of children in the group who stay at school for lunch, we say "one-third", or "more than half" or "almost three-quarters". Moreover, children become familiar with situations involving splitting into fractions when they are very young. Sharing often leads to situations involving fractions, where everybody gets half a strip of liquorice or one-third of a candy bar. By the time they are seven or eight, most children already know a number of simple fractions, even if these were not addressed in the arithmetic lessons.

The concept of a fraction links up closely with the way young children think. It is more of a basal concept than percentages or decimals. Fractions were already known to the Babylonians and the ancient Egyptians, and thousands of years ago in India, while percentages and decimals are recent inventions (see Chapter 2). If we skip fractions before we introduce decimals and percentages, we standardize things from the beginning. We start right away with tenths and hundredths, instead of introducing hundredths as fractions similar to thirds, quarters, fifths and so on. And we impose decimals immediately as a way of making smaller units, while doing this with fractions is more natural in many situations. When we start right away with percentages and decimals, we impose these concepts from above, without offering the children a chance to develop these concepts themselves.

How much should children know about fractions?

Fractions should be taught because understanding fractions is the foundation for arithmetic using percentages and decimals. This point of departure places limits on what children should be taught about fractions. For example, is it really necessary for children to be able to calculate "$\frac{1}{2} \times \frac{1}{3} =$", or is a global understanding of fractions sufficient? Or should children be able to solve problems such as "$\frac{2}{3} : \frac{1}{3} =$"?

It is not a simple matter to formulate exactly what children should understand or be able to do, because this primarily concerns the level at which they should know something or be able to do something. For example, children must know that one-sixth is one-half of one-third and that one-third fits twice into two-thirds. This is related to calculating sums such as "$\frac{1}{2} \times \frac{1}{3} =$" and "$\frac{2}{3} : \frac{1}{3} =$", but is certainly not the same thing. These sums require mastery of abstract mathematical procedures, while the relationship between sixths and thirds is really basic knowledge.

In this chapter on fractions, we will discuss the core insights that all children require. In Chapter 7, we will focus separately on the better students. After all, there are many children who can also handle fractions and operations with fractions on a higher, more abstract level, and who actually understand sums like "$\frac{1}{2} \times \frac{1}{3}$" and "$\frac{2}{3} : \frac{1}{3}$". In that chapter, we will also address the question of how we can offer a sufficient challenge to these better students.

Measuring

Situations with fractions can be - very roughly - divided into sharing and measuring situations. Fractions are created when a certain number of things are to be shared out and this number is not equal to the number of people who want to receive a share or to a multiple of the number of people. Fractions also result from the need for smaller measurements. There are half-litre cartons of milk, while cream is sold in quarter-litre and eighth-litre cartons. Refining by cutting in half every time seems to be obvious, although today the gradation in centilitres is indicated on every carton or cup. In the past, most people did not use decimal measurements; many kinds of fractions were used instead.

The difference between measuring situations and sharing situations is not absolute, because the result of sharing, can also be regarded as a measurement. When eight people share six pizzas, we can say that everybody gets "$\frac{3}{4}$ pizza". We are not concerned with exactly how the pizzas are cut; we use "pizza" as a unit of measurement.

Concrete material

When addressing difficult topics like fractions, we like to use concrete material, but sometimes this may pose a problem, as shown in the following example. To help them learn how to do arithmetic with fractions, the students have an activity sheet with fraction strips. They have cut out the strips and use these as measuring strips. The sum they are supposed to do is $\frac{1}{2} + \frac{1}{3} = ?$

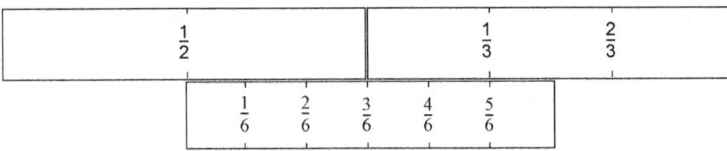

By manipulating the strips, Dennis comes up with $\frac{1}{2} + \frac{1}{3} = \frac{5}{6}$. The illustration shows how he places the strips above each other. Another student, Michael, also works with measuring strips, but ends up with $\frac{1}{2} + \frac{1}{3} = \frac{9}{11}$. At first glance, Michael seems to be working like Dennis. He measures $\frac{1}{2}$ plus $\frac{1}{3}$ using the measuring strips of halves and thirds, and then measures the result with a suitable measuring strip. However, Michael appears to be measuring literally. Because the strips were drawn accurately, his answer is almost right. Dennis, on the other hand, arrives at the exact answer. Is this a coincidence, or has Dennis done something essentially different?

It seems likely that Dennis was led by his knowledge of the relationships between the fraction strips: one piece of $\frac{1}{2}$ is exactly equal to three pieces of $\frac{1}{6}$, and one piece of $\frac{1}{3}$ is exactly equal to two pieces of $\frac{1}{6}$. Perhaps he found this solution by experimenting; he could have realized that he had the correct answer only after he found his solution. It is also possible that Dennis knew the answer immediately, and only used the strips to illustrate his solution.

To understand that $\frac{1}{2} + \frac{1}{3} = \frac{5}{6}$, students do not necessarily have to think about tangible objects or imaginary ones; it is also possible that the number relationships have become so familiar to them that thinking in terms of these relationships is sufficient. In order to get that far, students must be given the opportunity to develop a system of mathematical relationships. Merely measuring, like Michael does, does not contribute to that. Working with fraction strips can only contribute to the intended development if the teacher makes sure that the students test their solutions by explaining the relationships between the measurements they used. Good mathematics education involves more that the quality of the concrete materials; it also involves the quality of the students' discussions of the reasoning behind their solutions.

In this way, measuring offers a natural context for developing understanding of fractions. When using a strip for a measuring unit, if that strip turns out to be too big, an obvious solution is to make it smaller by folding it. By folding it repeatedly in half, you automatically get halves, quarters and eighths, but theoretically the strip can also be divided into thirds or fifths.

The notation with numerators larger than 1 origi-nated from measuring. The step from unit fractions - such as $\frac{1}{3}$, $\frac{1}{4}$ and $\frac{1}{5}$ - to fractions with larger nu-merators - such as $\frac{2}{3}$, $\frac{3}{4}$ and $\frac{2}{5}$ - is bigger than it may seem. In an every-day context, there is no immedi-ate need for such fractions, because you can man-age very well with the description "2 pieces of $\frac{1}{3}$". However, the notation $\frac{2}{3}$ makes it possible to view the fraction as a distinct number, separate from the act of sharing or dividing. The notation $\frac{2}{3}$ has a dou-ble meaning:

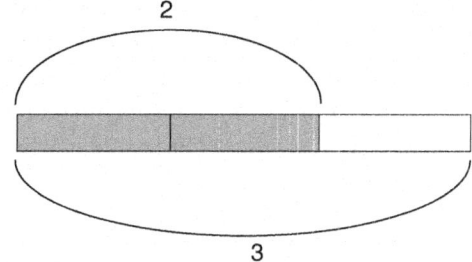

- $\frac{2}{3}$ represents an action. $\frac{2}{3}$ stands for "2 pieces of $\frac{1}{3}$", in which $\frac{1}{3}$ is the measurement.
- $\frac{2}{3}$ stands for the proportion "2 to 3", the relationship between part and whole.

Sharing

Situations involving sharing offer a different approach to developing un-derstanding about fractions. During sharing, fractions appear in various ways:

- When three people share something equally, everyone gets $\frac{1}{3}$ of the whole.
- A remainder can be left over, in which case everyone also has a right to part of the remainder; when 7 mandarins are shared equally between three people, everyone receives $2\frac{1}{3}$ mandarins.
- The process of "fair sharing" leads to a fraction: in case of three pan-cakes for four people, everybody gets $\frac{3}{4}$ pancake, so $3 : 4 = \frac{3}{4}$.

Making fraction strips

In order to make students think about finding the least common denominator of fractions, they can be asked to make fraction strips themselves. We designed a lesson about a baker who makes pastry bars and cuts these on the request of the customer. The assignment for the students is to think of a way to do this efficiently. For example, you can divide a pastry bar into six pieces by imagining that you can divide halves into three pieces, or you can first divide the bar into thirds and then cut each of the thirds in half. Another assignment is: "Describe how you would divide a pastry bar into twelve equal pieces".

During this lesson, the students make the transition from dealing with tangible strips to abstract reasoning. During their work, the students discover all kinds of fractional relationships.

A number of teachers have experimented with the lesson and report that it leads to many discoveries. For example, students learn that $\frac{1}{8}$ is smaller than $\frac{1}{4}$ and discover that $\frac{8}{8}$ is an entire pastry bar. They also discover that, in the case of $\frac{1}{15}$, you have to divide into thirds and then into fifths, or the other way around. They also see that it has something to do with tables.

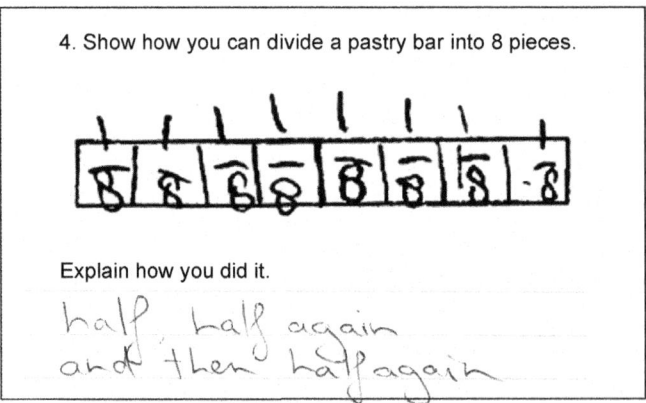

4. Show how you can divide a pastry bar into 8 pieces.

Explain how you did it.

half half again and then half again

In the case of $\frac{1}{15}$, the insight that you can first divide something into thirds and then into fifths forms the basis for the assumption that $\frac{1}{5} = \frac{3}{15}$, because $\frac{1}{15}$ is three times smaller than $\frac{1}{5}$. This leads to reasoning about equivalent relations. Students can use familiar number relationships. For the time being, however, the students refer to fifteen pieces, and not fifteenths.

Later on in this chapter, we will elaborate more on situations involving sharing. At this point we will mention that besides the typical sharing situations, other situations should also be discussed, like dividing these two apples between four people. In measurement terms, you could say that "apple" is not a suitable unit of measurement in this case. It is wise to choose a two-track approach and to explore both measuring and sharing situations with the students.

Developing a network of relationships

Labelled and unlabelled fractions

In a context situation, a fraction always refers to a specific part of something:

- Part of one thing: a gas tank is $\frac{3}{4}$ full, $\frac{3}{4}$ of a cake has been eaten.
- Part of a set or collection: $\frac{3}{4}$ of the children have dark hair.
- Part of a certain quantity: a 40-litre tank is still $\frac{3}{4}$ full, $\frac{3}{4}$ of the group of 20 children are present.
- Part of a measurement unit: $\frac{3}{4}$ kilometre, $\frac{3}{4}$ hour.

Part/whole proportions are always involved. This is also the case for $\frac{3}{2}$, a fraction larger than 1; in a context situation, the $\frac{1}{2}$ that is left over is the issue. Fractions are proportion numbers; this means that it has to be clear to everyone what proportion is involved. We often do not make an explicit reference, because the context already shows exactly what we mean. However, this may lead children to conclude that $\frac{3}{4}$ or $\frac{1}{3}$ do not refer to anything specific. For example, we can easily confuse them by saying:

> Achmed, Joost and Tessa order two pizzas together and divide them up between the three of them. Do they each get $\frac{1}{3}$ or $\frac{3}{2}$?

In order to emphasize the relative character of fractions, it is advisable to have the children work with labelled fraction problems as much as possible at first, which means that the students write down explicitly what every fraction refers to. In case of a problem about pizzas, they write "$\frac{3}{4}$ pizza = $\frac{1}{2}$ pizza + $\frac{1}{4}$ pizza" instead of "$\frac{3}{4} = \frac{1}{2} + \frac{1}{4}$".

There is a second reason for having the children explicitly label every fraction at first. Notation like "$\frac{3}{4} = \frac{1}{2} + \frac{1}{4}$" erroneously suggests that children are already able to reason on an abstract, formal level, where fractions are separate from the context. Initially, however, the children's reasoning is strongly connected to the context.

A network of relationships around fractions

Eventually, children also have to develop knowledge that is separate from tangible situations. For example, they will have to understand that $\frac{1}{2} + \frac{1}{4}$ is $\frac{3}{4}$, whether it concerns pizzas, litres or numbers of children. They will have to understand, without any context, that $\frac{3}{4}$ is larger than $\frac{2}{3}$. They will have to be able to reason that $\frac{4}{5}$ is smaller than $\frac{5}{6}$, for example by looking at what remains relative to the whole: $\frac{1}{5}$ and $\frac{1}{6}$. This is all knowledge about unlabelled fractions, removed from the tangible context; this is why it can be applied generally. However, this does not mean that the link with tangible situations has disappeared. The children should be able to imagine situations themselves that "prove" that an answer is correct, and they should be able to support this reasoning with a drawing, for example of a bar or a circle. They should also be able to give examples of what such a bar or circle represents. The knowledge that children develop about the relations between different types of fractions is called a "network of relationships". In all probability, students at the end of fourth grade have reasonable knowledge about simple fractions like one-half, one-third and one-quarter. During the fifth and sixth grades, their knowledge about fractions expands more and more, and gradually reaches a higher, more formal level. Eventually, children can reason as follows:

"$\frac{3}{4}$ is less than $\frac{4}{5}$, because with $\frac{3}{4}$, you have $\frac{1}{4}$ left over, and with $\frac{4}{5}$, you have $\frac{1}{5}$ left over. So you have less left over with $\frac{4}{5}$."

This knowledge is no longer linked to specific context situations, but it still is knowledge about specific fractions. A student who can reason that $\frac{3}{4}$ is less than $\frac{4}{5}$, is not necessarily able to reason that $\frac{14}{15}$ is less than $\frac{15}{16}$.
Children do not develop a network of relationships around fractions simply by practicing a lot. If the emphasis is on purely numerical fraction problems (without context), there is a high probability that the children will begin using calculation rules that they do not understand. It is much better to develop the network of relationships from context situations - from situations with labelled fractions.

Dividing cleverly

With fractions, the issue is always to share or divide in a very specific way: the pieces or parts all have to be equal in size. Young children sometimes find it difficult to make a "fair" division of pieces. If they are asked to cut a pizza into four pieces, they sometimes do that as shown here.

Dividing a strip into equal pieces is also much more difficult for young children than we are inclined to think. When they are asked to divide a drawing of a baguette into six equal parts, they often do this as shown here. They work from left to right and get in trouble because they make the first parts too big. Even in this case, however, the child has noticed that you only have to make five divisions to get six pieces!

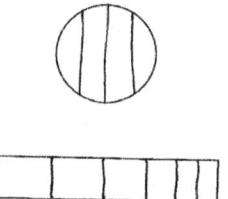

In education, there should be plenty of space to allow the children to discover "fair sharing". When students investigate the geometry of fair sharing, they also investigate the relationships between fractions. For example, you can divide a strip into six pieces by first finding "half" and then dividing each half into three pieces. In terms of fractions, this means: $\frac{1}{2} = \frac{1}{6} + \frac{1}{6} + \frac{1}{6}$. In the same way, discussing clever ways of dividing also brings up the relationships between other fractions. Such activities are discussed in the box on page 72.

Sharing more than one object equally

Situations in which more than one object has to be shared are also suitable for investigating the relationships between fractions. There are various ways in which four children can divide three pizzas. Several of these ways are illustrated here. In every situation, each child gets $\frac{3}{4}$. From the various ways of dividing, it turns out that you can say:

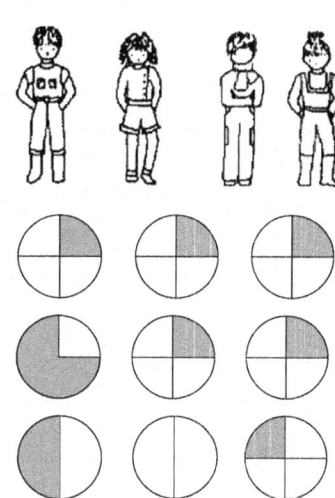

$\frac{3}{4}$ pizza $= \frac{1}{4}$ pizza $+ \frac{1}{4}$ pizza $+ \frac{1}{4}$ pizza

$\frac{3}{4}$ pizza $= 1 - \frac{1}{4}$ pizza

$\frac{3}{4}$ pizza $= \frac{1}{2}$ pizza $+ \frac{1}{4}$ pizza

Here are a few more examples of slightly more complicated sharing situations and the insights that emerge from them.

Sharing four things between five people:

Sharing pizzas

Students are asked how they would share two pizzas between three people. Kofi says he would give everyone $\frac{1}{2}$ pizza plus $\frac{1}{6}$ pizza. The teacher asks how you can draw that on the worksheet. Stacey has an idea. He divides both circles in half, and then he divides one of the halves into three.

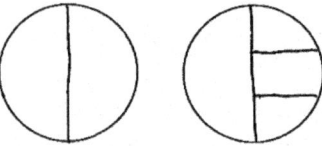

Stacey's solution

Eva has a different solution. She also starts with halves, but after that she divides one of the two halves into 6 parts.

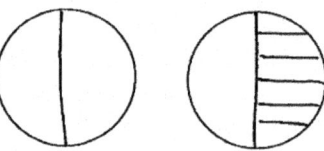

Eva's solution

The teacher asks whether everyone agrees with Eva's method. Cesar explains what went wrong: the small parts are not sixths, but twelfths. Eva disagrees. They are sixths, because there are six parts, right? Not everybody seems to understand what is wrong with Eva's logic.

The teacher then asks the group how you can make sixths. This turns out to be a difficult question, but Cesar is able to explain. He uses his turn to provide his entire solution.

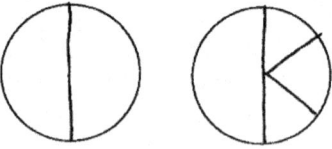

Cesar's solution

Cesar explains why the parts are sixths. One whole pizza holds six of those parts.

$$\tfrac{4}{5} = \tfrac{1}{5} + \tfrac{1}{5} + \tfrac{1}{5} + \tfrac{1}{5} = 4 \times \tfrac{1}{5}$$

$$\tfrac{4}{5} = 1 - \tfrac{1}{5}$$

$$\tfrac{4}{5} = \tfrac{1}{2} + \tfrac{1}{5} + \tfrac{1}{10} \quad \tfrac{4}{5} = \tfrac{1}{2} + \tfrac{3}{10}$$

$$\tfrac{4}{5} = \tfrac{5}{10} + \tfrac{3}{10} = \tfrac{8}{10}$$

Sharing six things between eight people:

$$\tfrac{6}{8} = \tfrac{1}{8} + \tfrac{1}{8} + \tfrac{1}{8} + \tfrac{1}{8} + \tfrac{1}{8} + \tfrac{1}{8} = 6 \times \tfrac{1}{8}$$

$$\tfrac{6}{8} = \tfrac{1}{2} + \tfrac{1}{4} = 3 \times \tfrac{1}{4} = \tfrac{3}{4}$$

Sharing five things between six people

$$\tfrac{5}{6} = \tfrac{1}{6} + \tfrac{1}{6} + \tfrac{1}{6} + \tfrac{1}{6} + \tfrac{1}{6} = 5 \times \tfrac{1}{6}$$

$$\tfrac{5}{6} = \tfrac{1}{3} + \tfrac{1}{3} + \tfrac{1}{6} = \tfrac{2}{3} + \tfrac{1}{6}$$

$$\tfrac{5}{6} = \tfrac{1}{2} + \tfrac{1}{3}$$

$$\tfrac{5}{6} = 1 - \tfrac{1}{6}$$

It is important to realize that all these sharing problems are concerned with reasoning, and not about determining the result empirically. From the perspective of the sharing situation, these relationships seem logical to the children. By investigating the sharing situations, the children develop a network of relationships around fractions that enables them to do arithmetic with fractions, but without requiring them to learn explicit arithmetic rules. This is enough for the students for a long time. They will learn about generally applicable arithmetic procedures later on.

Measuring with a strip

With measuring, fractions are required when the measuring unit does not fit and we still want to describe the outcome accurately. The most natural solution seems to be to repeatedly cut items in half.

When you take half and it still does not add up, you can take half again, and again if need be. Students do this spontaneously, for example when we have them measure all sorts of things in class with a paper strip they can fold. During this process, they may describe a quarter as "half of a half".

Measuring with an "Amsterdam foot"

The students are measuring the length of their tables with a strip that is equivalent to an "Amsterdam foot". The teacher abbreviates this unit as "AF". Some of the students state that their tables are "two AF and one-half AF" long. Eva is more precise: she says her table is "two and three quarters AF long". The teacher follows up with more questions: "How can you fold a strip so you can see if Eva is right?" Rianne tries, but ends up with a strip that is folded in three. The teacher asks her what a piece like that is called. She knows the answer: it is one-third.

The teacher returns to the original problem. One of the students now sees how you can make a strip that you can use to measure "three-fourths": he folds the strip in fourths and shows how long three-fourths is.

Who is taller? Why do you think so?

Roel is taller, because
I don't know.

Roel, because
5 AF. is taller
than 4 AF

Roel, because
He is taller.

Roel, because
5/4 AF is tall.

The children also use the Amsterdam foot to compare how tall they are. On the activity sheet, it says that Roel is $5\frac{1}{4}$ AF tall and that Lonneke is $4\frac{3}{4}$ AF tall.

Stacey thinks Roel is taller, but he can't explain why. He can only say: "Well,… because he is taller." Anoek probably does understand what is going on, but has difficulty expressing her thoughts. She says: "Roel says he is five and Lonneke says she is four, and here it says one-fourth and there three-fourths".

Kevin says: "5 AF is taller than 4 AF." He leaves out the fractions. Finally, Eva comes up with an argument that the teacher accepts: "Roel is 5 AF and some more, and Lonneke is more than 4, but still less than 5".

When the students are already somewhat familiar with the language of fractions, other denominators can also start to play a role. The teacher can introduce pre-structured strips (or bars) that have already been divided into a certain number of pieces. The students can then choose different strips to see which subdivision works best for a measurement. In one case, for example, the strip of sixths will have the best fit, and a length may turn out to be three-and-five-sixths of a measuring strip.

Models for reasoning with fractions

Bar and number line

In a context problem, a fraction is a certain part of something, and that "something" is often a quantity. When we refer to "one-fourth of the Dutch population", this is approximately equal to "one-fourth of 16 million people". We are therefore talking about two relationships at the same time: the relationship between one-fourth and a whole, and the relation between 4 million and 16 million. A bar can represent that double relationship very accurately.

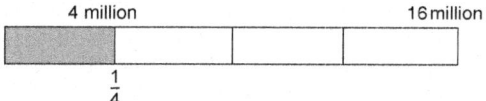

Dials on control panels have the same double meaning. On the fuel gauge on the left, everyone sees that the tank is three-fourths full, but if you know that the tank holds 40 litres, you can also understand that there are 30 litres left. This double meaning also appears on both a bar and a double number line.

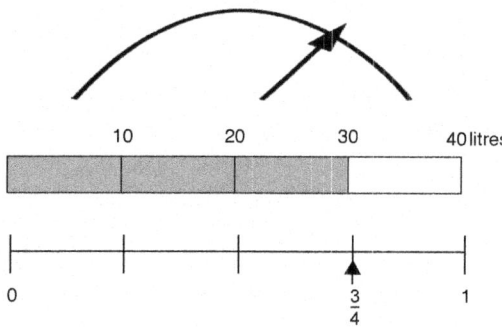

Computer programs with fractions

With the computer program "Fair Sharing" ("Eerlijk Verdelen"), the students investigate sharing situations, for example how four children can share three slices of cake between them, or how three children can share seven Mars bars. All cutting methods are allowed, including diagonally or crosswise. After they are cut, the pieces can be shared out. The piece that is given to a girl in a red shirt then turns red, and so on. The program checks whether the total that every child gets corresponds with a fair share.

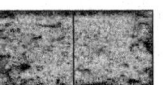 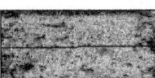

The piece of cheese pictured here weighs 4000 grams. Students are asked to slice off a piece that weighs 500 grams. With the computer program, "Slicing off" ("Afsnijden"), they can cut slices by drawing lines. In this case, help lines come in handy: first draw a line that cuts the cheese in half (2000 grams), then in half (1000 grams) and then in half again (500 grams). The program encourages students to use fractions in proportion situations.

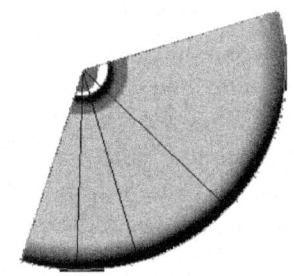

The same goes for the "Cloud Train". In this assignment, the pointer on the dial in the picture must be set to 40; the entire scale (the dial) goes from 0 to 60. A possible argument is that the scale at the bottom, which is halfway, indicates 30, and that 45 would be three-quarters of the way around. The pointer must be placed somewhere between the two, but closer to 45 than to 30. Another argument is that 20 of 60 is $\frac{1}{3}$, so the pointer must be placed at $\frac{2}{3}$ of the way around. Of course, a dial with a scale of 60 could also suggest a clock face. Implicitly, this involves a double number line, with numbers on one side and fractions on the other side.

The computer programs can be found at www.rekenweb.nl.

Children can work especially well with the bar as a model, because they can easily use it to illustrate part-whole reasoning. The double number line is more abstract; the "whole" is just a dot on the line. The fact that this dot refers to a length quickly fades into the background, especially when the beginning of the number line is not shown, as in the illustration on the right. We can also use the bar when comparing measurements. The entire bar is not only 1 meter long, but it is also 100 cm at the same time.

When children know that $4 \times 25 = 100$, they can convert $\frac{3}{4}$ meter to 75 cm.

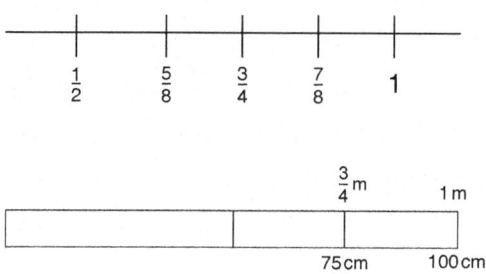

The circle

Of course, the circle plays a role in teaching fractions. The time when fractions were explained by using wooden circles that were divided into separate segments is behind us, but nowadays the pizza and the pancake have taken their place. One advantage of the circle is that the orientation of the lines gives the parts their own character. Everyone can see, probably without drawing help lines, that the first picture represents $\frac{1}{3}$ and the second one $\frac{3}{8}$. This is not as easy to see with bars. This is probably why the pie chart is so widely used to illustrate election returns, for example so readers can see the results "at a glance". However, although a circle may be easier to interpret as an illustration, it can be more difficult to use as a conceptual model. With a bar, it is much easier for us to disregard precise drawing, as long as the correct numbers are attached. Although the pieces in the illustration are totally out of proportion, the meaning is still clear.

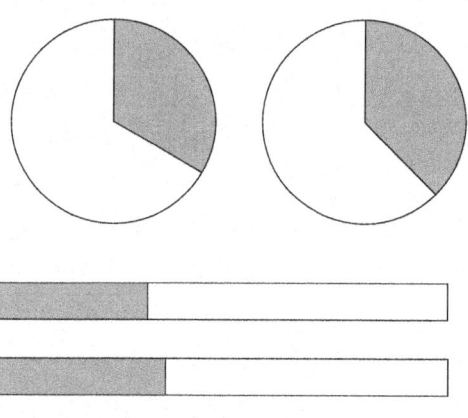

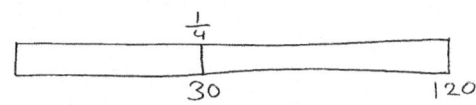

Doing arithmetic with fractions

Comparing fractions

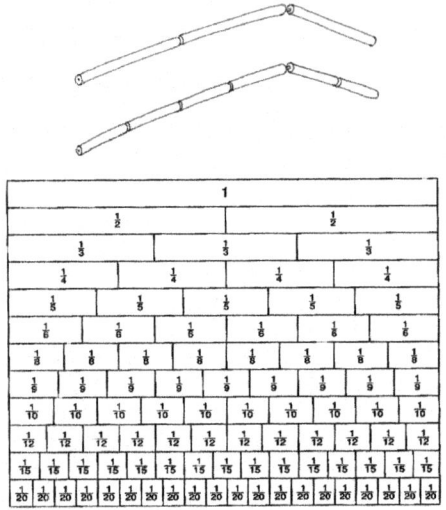

Children must be able to compare simple fractions and say which one is bigger. They also have to be able to work out why two fractions are "equally big". This process explicitly involves reasoning, not memorization. The danger of materials like "fraction sticks" and the so-called "fraction cupboard" is that the students take what they see for a standard.

Measuring precisely with strips leads children to conclude that $\frac{2}{3}$ is equal to $\frac{4}{6}$. But why is $\frac{2}{3}$ exactly as long as $\frac{4}{6}$? Children who do not get any further with this question than "you can just see it" will probably conclude that the two fractions are not equal if they measure less precisely with strips. Comparing fractions must therefore be based on reasoning. For example:

"If you divide a strip into three parts, you get thirds. In order to get six equal parts, you have to divide every part in two again. So one piece of one-third is two-sixths and two of those pieces are four-sixths."

Strips and bars, therefore, must be used as a conceptual model. The exact lengths are not important; what matters is that drawing such a strip helps children to reason logically. They do not all progress at the same rate with this type of reasoning. For example, children who understand fractions abstractly, and who can reason on a fairly high, formal level, will be able to reason why $\frac{1}{3}$ is smaller than $\frac{3}{8}$.

"$\frac{1}{3}$ is the same as $\frac{3}{9}$. Ninths are smaller than eighths, so $\frac{3}{9}$ is smaller than $\frac{3}{8}$. $\frac{1}{3}$ is smaller than $\frac{3}{8}$."

Other children will only be able to use such reasoning with simpler fractions such as thirds and fourths.

"You get $\frac{1}{3}$ when you divide a strip in three equal parts, $\frac{1}{4}$ when you divide a strip in four parts. So $\frac{1}{3}$ is bigger than $\frac{1}{4}$."

The question is, how familiar are the children with certain fractions? Nearly all students in grades 5 and 6 can reason with fractions using thirds and fourths, because they have a very tangible understanding of thirds and fourths. But only some of these children are so familiar with the world of fractions that eighths and ninths have become as real to them as thirds and fourths.

Adding and subtracting fractions

At the beginning of this chapter, we stated that knowledge of fractions is important especially as a foundation for understanding percentages and decimals. By itself, being able to do arithmetic with fractions has limited practical value. Consequently, with respect to the skills the children must learn, there is only a modest need for exercises in fraction arithmetic.

As stated previously, children must be able to compare fractions in terms of size, although for some of the children this can remain limited to reasoning on a fairly concrete level and with simple fractions. Adding and subtracting can also be limited largely to reasoning in a tangible context. In the section about developing a network of relations, we described how fair sharing can lead to a series of sums that describe the shared result. To go a step further, addition and subtraction are based primarily on finding the least common denominator; thirds and fourths, for example, can only be added to or subtracted from each other by making them into twelfths. When students can compare fractions by finding the common denominator, it is only a small step to adding and subtracting those fractions.

As an aid towards routine addition and subtraction with fractions, we can use what Treffers calls a "sub-unit".[1] For example: when students have to calculate the difference between $\frac{3}{4}$ and $\frac{2}{3}$ of a candy bar, it would be convenient if this bar happened to consist of 12 pieces. Using these "pieces" as the unit of measurement, the approach changes to the subtraction problem (9-8 pieces), after which the sub-unit can be converted back to the original unit (candy bar): "nine pieces minus eight pieces is one piece, so the answer is $\frac{1}{12}$ candy bar". In some cases, students can devise a suitable sub-unit themselves.

Recipes with fractions

Proportion tables for recipes offer an interesting way of investigating multiplying and dividing with fractions. A proportion table is attractive because the results can be compared to numbers in other segments in many different ways. From the viewpoint of teaching, it is therefore unfortunate that modern European cookbooks indicate ingredients in grams or centilitres, and usually not in cups or tablespoons. These measurements are used in older cookbooks and are still very common in British and American cook books.

In an American cookbook for children, we found a recipe for "yogurt cups". The assignment for the children was to convert the recipe for 4 servings into recipes for 2, 6, 8 and 16 servings.

servings	4	2	8	6	10	16
flour (cups)	$\frac{3}{4}$					
margarine (cups)	$\frac{1}{4}$					
powdered sugar (tablespoons)	3					
water (teaspoons)	$2\frac{1}{2}$					
yogurt (cups)	$1\frac{1}{3}$					

While filling in the table, the children have to decide what is half of a certain fraction and what is twice that fraction. For other columns, they need to add or subtract.

In a somewhat more formal approach, a segmented strip can serve as model. At the start of the activity, paper strips are available that have been divided into a large number of sections (segments). Choosing a sub-unit here involves determining the length of the strip you are cutting off. In this example, five pieces have to be coloured in to represent $\frac{1}{4}$ of a strip of 20 segments.

This activity can be replaced with a more schematic representation, which can then be used as a durable, conceptual model.

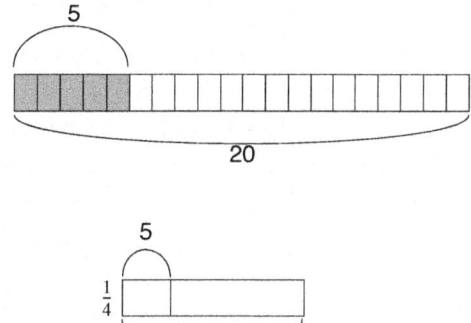

Multiplying with fractions

As long as multiplication with fractions can be understood as repeated addition, students have little trouble:

- "Four people eat $\frac{3}{4}$ pizza each" ($4 \times \frac{3}{4} = \frac{12}{4}$, which is 3 pizzas).
- "A stack of three boxes; every box is $\frac{3}{4}$ meters tall."
  ($3 \times \frac{3}{4} = 2\frac{1}{4}$, meaning 2 m and 25 cm).

These are situations in which a whole number is multiplied by a fraction. Situations in which the fraction would be the multiplier are not recognized by the children as a multiplication problem:

- "Apples cost € 2.00 per kilo. How much would you pay for $\frac{3}{4}$ of a kilo?"
- "You need $\frac{3}{4}$ meters of fabric. The fabric costs € 8.00 per meter."

In a context situation, students can probably handle these two problems, but if the numbers become so difficult that the children have to use a calculator, things can go wrong. For example:

- "Apples cost €1.15 per kilo. How much would you pay for $\frac{3}{4}$ of a kilo?"
- "You need $\frac{3}{4}$ meters of fabric. The fabric costs € 8.50 per meter."

This involves multiplying a fraction with a whole number. Most students understand that $\frac{3}{4}$ is equal to 0.75, but the step towards "0.75 × *something*" is quite a big one.

Enlargement factor

In order to give meaning to multiplication problems like "$2\frac{2}{5} \times 6$", we designed a lesson based on enlarging photographs.

How many times have the pictures a, b, and c been enlarged?

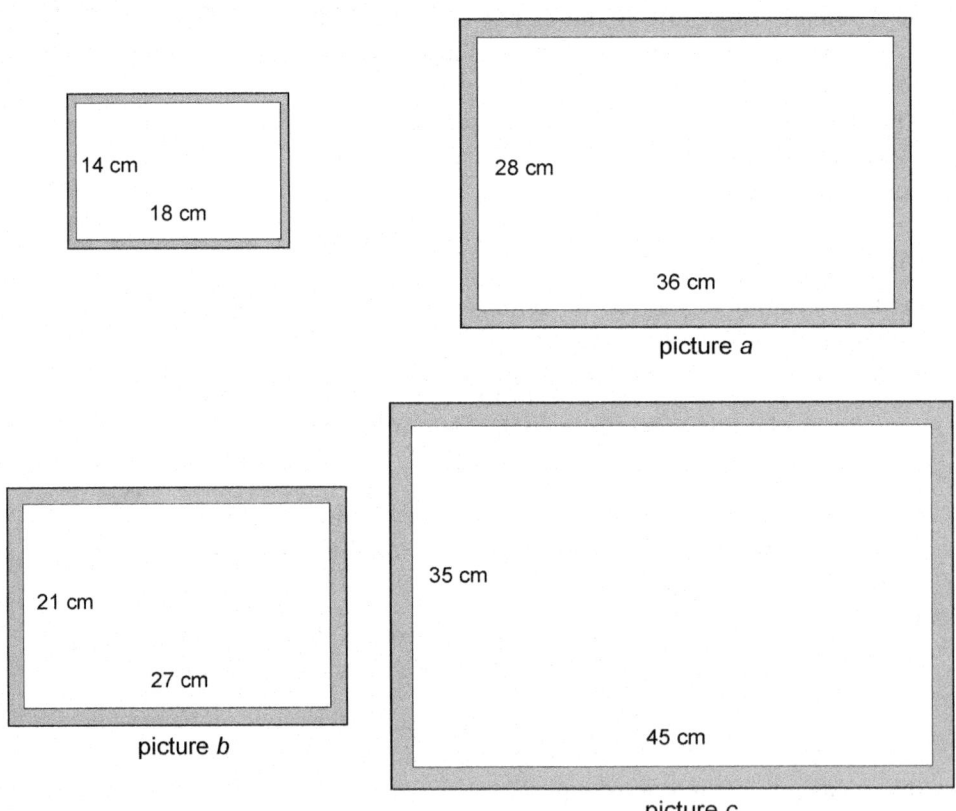

14 cm
18 cm

28 cm
36 cm

picture a

21 cm
27 cm

picture b

35 cm
45 cm

picture c

Students are encouraged to reason in terms like "twice as big". They eventually move on to concepts such as "one-and-a-half times as big". As a result, multiplying with a fraction is given meaning as an enlargement factor. Eventually, the situation is turned around: students can propose other frame sizes and use a certain enlargement factor, which they can set themselves, as their starting point.

Reducing a picture can be dealt with in the same way. Consequently, a meaning can be given to multiplication problems like $\frac{1}{2} \times 20$, where one of the factors is smaller than 1.

Multiplying with fractions is especially difficult because students associate multiplying with making something larger. It seems strange to them that the result of $\frac{3}{4} \times 1.15$ is actually smaller than 1.15, and that the result of 0.75×8.50 is smaller than 8.50.

It is difficult for the children to interpret "a certain fraction of something" as multiplication. This problem often disappears when they can relate this to multiplying with whole numbers, for example by solving problems with mixed numbers. The amount you have to pay in the supermarket for two kilos of peaches that cost € 3.50 per kilo can be calculated with 2×3.50. From here, the children can make the step to figuring the cost of $2\frac{1}{2}$ kilos as 2.5×3.50. At first, the children interpret that as "twice, plus half." The teacher must show explicitly that this problem can also be read as "$2\frac{1}{2}$ times 3.50". We will get back at this when we discuss multiplying with decimals. Length and width can also be mixed numbers when working in the context of calculating areas. In Chapter 7 on differentiation, an activity regarding the area of a small tile floor will be discussed.

Not only do students have difficulty converting context problems with fractions into a multiplication problem, they also have difficulty with purely numerical fraction problems. In this regard, "$\frac{3}{4} \times 2$" is a difficult problem because children cannot give a meaning to "$\frac{3}{4}$ times something". This is also caused by the fact that they understand multiplication almost exclusively from situations involving repeated addition, and "$\frac{3}{4}$ times something" cannot be interpreted as repeated addition.

We can do two things to give meaning to problems like $\frac{3}{4} \times 2$. First, it is a good idea to have the students look at these multiplication problems on a more formal level, in this case by discussing the commutativity principle. In multiplication, you can switch the terms around without affecting the result. The students are more familiar with notation such as $2 \times \frac{3}{4}$, but then they understand that this is the same as $\frac{3}{4} \times 2$.

The fact that 18×5 has the same outcome as 5×18 seems natural to children in grades 3-6, perhaps so natural that they do not see any difference between the two multiplication problems. However, when working with concrete situations, 18 bags of 5 raisin buns is a completely different thing than 5 bags of 18 raisin buns. Children have to be made aware that something weird is indeed happening: two different situations can be described with the same multiplication problem. Consequently, you can also figure

5×18 in two ways; not only by adding $18 + 18 + 18 + 18 + 18$, but also by adding $5 + 5 + 5 + 5 + 5 + 5 + 5 + 5$. Commutativity is not self-evident because switching terms is possible in multiplication and addition, but not in subtraction and division.

Another way to give multiplying with a fraction a meaning is to make sure that students understand multiplication as more than just repeated addition. A multiplication problem can also be a factor. In a drawing with a scale of 1:8, everything is 8 times larger in reality than in the drawing. This "8x" is an enlargement factor that you can apply to all dimensions in the drawing. The important thing is the proportion, not repeated addition; all the dimensions in the drawing are eight times longer in reality. Viewed another way, each dimension in the drawing is $\frac{1}{8}$ of its length in reality. Activities involving scale and enlargement are suitable for broadening the concept of multiplication. An enlargement factor does not have to be a whole number. Instead of making a picture frame 2 times larger in length and width, we can also make it $2\frac{1}{2}$ or $2\frac{3}{4}$ times as large. We can also make the frame $\frac{3}{4}$ as big. The box on page 82, contains a discussion of a lesson about enlargement.

Dividing

In dividing - similar to multiplying - a fraction divided by a whole number has much more meaning for students than a whole number divided by a fraction. An important reason for this is that students associate dividing with "making smaller". This association applies correctly to the case of $\frac{1}{2} : 2$, because the fraction you get is smaller than the original one. In the case of $2 : \frac{1}{2}$, this association does not apply, because you end up with a larger number than the 2 you started out with.

Serving lemonade or coffee is a suitable context situation for discussing the process of making things smaller or larger. If you have a pitcher holding 2 litres of lemonade, you can pour 8 large glasses of $\frac{1}{4}$ litre each, so $2 : \frac{1}{4} = 8$. You can view the problem as repeated subtraction: how many times does $\frac{1}{4}$ fit into 8? One problem with this strategy, however, is that most students are more likely to solve the problem by thinking of multiplication ($8 \times \frac{1}{4} = 2$) than of division.

But is this really objectionable? Should students be able to solve various division problems with fractions, or is it sufficient if they understand division mainly as the opposite of multiplying?

We choose the latter approach, which means that numerical division (non-context problems) with fractions has to be practiced only to a limited extent. But this explicitly applies only to division with fractions, because dividing with decimals on the pocket calculator is a skill that the students are required to have mastered.

As in multiplication, students should not associate division only with repeated subtraction, but also with describing a proportion. There is a good reason why we use the division sign (:) to indicate the scale of a drawing or map. A map with a scale of 1 : 50,000 means that every centimetre is 50,000 cm in reality, or half a kilometre, and that every distance on the map is $\frac{1}{5000}$ part of the real distance. In this case, you do not divide with a fraction, but you use fractions to define a ratio.

The global learning-teaching trajectory

We hesitate to speak of a learning-teaching trajectory for fractions here, because in this book we try to emphasize that fractions, percentages, decimals and proportions should not be considered separate trajectories. The characterization of the learning-teaching trajectory we offer here should be interpreted from that perspective. As in the chapter on proportion, we will describe a number of sub-trajectories.

Developing language about fractions

When students arrive in grade 4, they already know about fractions in an informal way - as one-half, one-quarter and so on - but they have not yet gone deeply into fractions. The process begins with a systematic exploration of situations in which fractions occur. During this exploration, the language about fractions must be carefully developed. Sharing offers a good opportunity for this, because sharing situations lead to all kinds of fractions. An important step in developing this language is the transformation of a "certain part of" into a measurement unit. For example, at first we refer to "one-sixth of a pastry bar" and later on to "$\frac{1}{6}$ pastry bar". This is followed by the expansion to fractions with numerators that are not equal to 1, where $\frac{5}{6}$ stands for five times $\frac{1}{6}$ pastry bar. It is important that students wean themselves from making and counting parts as soon as possible. They must start to see fractions as descriptions of part-whole proportions, in which $\frac{2}{5}$ refers to the proportion "2 out of 5". Based on that proportion, the students can understand that $\frac{2}{5}$ is smaller than $\frac{1}{2}$.

They may think of a strip that looks like this:

This interpretation of $\frac{2}{5}$ as a relationship between part and whole is exactly what we are aiming for during measuring when we describe a remainder. An example is shown below, where the measurement unit fits into the length $2\frac{2}{5}$ times.

Finding the common denominator by reasoning

Division is also used to prepare students for finding the common denominator. This takes place by discussing how you can best divide a pastry bar. The best way to divide into sixths is to first split the pastry bar in half, and then divide both halves into three If you have a circular cake, you might prefer to begin by dividing it into three parts. Investigating the relationships between dividing into sixths, thirds and halves prepares students for finding the common denominator of sixths, thirds and halves.

While engaging in "reasoned sharing", the students are actually preparing for multiplication and division as well; this takes place when we ask how many times one-sixth fits into one-half, or what you get when you put two pieces of one-sixth together.

Number relationships

Students develop number relationships mostly during activities involving fair sharing. They can work on this individually - for example with the computer program "Fair Sharing" - but there is also a need for class activities in which the students discuss their findings and the strategies they used.

Performing reasoned operations

When performing operations with fractions, two routes are followed: performing operations using reasoning (reasoned operations) and developing number relationships. Reasoning with fractions leads to the development of number relationships, but should also offer a way out if the students cannot readily find any number relationships.

Reasoned addition and subtraction builds upon finding the common denominator through reasoning. The objective is to have the children reason time and again about how finding the common denominator actually works. With multiplication, we distinguish situations that can be easily interpreted as repeated addition, and situations where that would be problematic. Multiplication as repeated addition builds on reasoned addition, just like repeated subtraction is a logical expansion of reasoned subtraction. In the following section we will discuss the more problematic situation, which involves the link between "part of" and "times".

Aside from reasoned multiplication and reasoned division, these operations also appear in more informal ways. For example, in "$\frac{2}{3}$ of 4500 kilos", or in "$\frac{3}{4}$ of 1 litre of water" - which can be solved with a double strip. These reasoned operations can also be found more implicitly by calculating the cost of 750 grams at € 1.20 per kilo by taking half of 1.20 plus "one-half of the half".

"Times"

Relating "part of" to "times" is a difficult problem. After all, the aim is to change and expand the image of what multiplication is. This image has been established over many years, and it is therefore unlikely that a brief explanation or a few lessons will offer a solution. This is why this theme must be addressed regularly and in different ways.

Encouraging the development of procedures

Being able to perform operations more routinely is considered to be an advanced skill for some of the students. However, this does not mean that activities that prepare students for such procedures should be left until the end of primary school or only addressed in groups of specially selected students. The thinking and the models that form the core of these activities are worthwhile for every student. For addition and subtraction, we have shown how the idea of a sub-unit and a schematic representation of segmented strips could work. With multiplication, tile floors can be used as the model. The example on page 136 in Chapter 7 shows how a small tile floor of $2\frac{1}{2}$ tiles wide by $3\frac{3}{4}$ tiles long can be converted into a floor of 5×15 smaller tiles, with a unit of $\frac{1}{2} \times \frac{1}{4}$ tile.

This establishes the foundation for the insight that $2\frac{1}{2} \times 3\frac{3}{4} = 15 \times \frac{1}{2} \times \frac{1}{4}$, because $2\frac{1}{2} = 5 \times \frac{1}{2}$ and $3\frac{3}{4} = 15 \times \frac{1}{4}$.

Performing division operations routinely can be supported by the idea of equality of division and by eliminating the fractions. According to this reasoning, $2\frac{1}{2} : 3\frac{3}{4}$ equals $10 : 15 = 2 : 3 = \frac{2}{3}$.

note

1 Treffers, A. (1994). *Proeve van een nationaal programma voor het reken-wiskundeonderwijs op de basisschool. Deel 3: Breuken.* Tilburg: Zwijsen.

5 Core insights into percentages

Percentages offer a standardized way of describing proportions. Their kinship with fractions, proportions and decimals provides many possibilities to do arithmetic in a flexible fashion. When estimating with percentages, simple fractions play an important role as reference points. When doing arithmetic on the calculator, the relationship with decimals plays a major role. The process of proportional reasoning can, as with proportions and fractions, be supported by using the double bar and the ratio table.

A scale from 0 to 100

During the course of history, percentages have become more popular than regular fractions. If you look in the newspaper, only very simple fractions such as "$\frac{1}{3}$", "$\frac{1}{4}$" and "$\frac{3}{4}$" are frequently used. The biggest disadvantage of fractions is that they are so difficult to compare with each other. For example, is $\frac{4}{5}$ larger or smaller than $\frac{2}{3}$? A student in grade 6 must be able to answer this question, but it is much more difficult than the question: is 80% larger or smaller than 67%?"

Percentages are numbers on a fixed scale that runs from 0 to 100. It is not coincidental that the scale goes to 100, instead of 75 for example. This is because in this way it is possible to place percentages neatly into our number system so that we can easily convert them into decimals. Moreover, a scale from 0 to 100 is one with which we are very familiar. When we see the figure "64%", most people have a clear image of how much that is with respect to the whole; it is more than half, but not that much more. The scale from 0 to 100 is precise enough for most situations. A system of "tenths" would also be compatible with our number system, but is rather unrefined. For situations where percentages in turn are too unrefined we can - due to their linkage with our number system - effortlessly make them more precise by adding more decimals to the right of the decimal point, or we can switch to "tenths of percent".

The introduction of percentages

Before percentages were introduced

In view of the relationship between percentages and fractions, it is desirable that children are already familiar with "hundredths" in normal fractional notation when percentages are introduced. After all, we want the concept of "one-hundredth" to have meaning for children. This does not happen if we only refer to fractions such as "thirds" and "eighths" in grade 4, and we thereafter introduce the concept of "one-hundredth" using totally different notation. The students must already have worked with fractions such as $\frac{20}{100}$ and $\frac{25}{100}$, and they must be able to explain, for example, why such fractions are equal to $\frac{1}{5}$ or $\frac{1}{4}$.

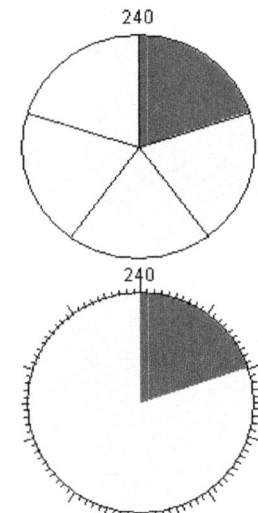

The computer program "In Kaart" ("Circles and bars", see box on page 90) can play a useful role in this regard. The program draws bars and circle diagrams when data are entered. It also provides the possibility to place a fractional division onto the circle diagram so that the students can search for a description in fractional terms. For example, if you click on $\frac{1}{5}$, the circle diagram is divided into five equal sections. If you click on $\frac{1}{100}$, the circle diagram becomes divided into 100 sections.

Initially, the students will perhaps not get any further than ascertaining that $\frac{20}{100}$ and $\frac{1}{5}$ fit into the same part of the circle diagram and are therefore "equal". The teacher must then shift the discussion and have the students try to explain why the fractions are equal.

Two approaches to introducing percentages

The introduction of percentages often takes place using the example of discount percentages. A justification for this is that the children are already familiar with the context of sales and discounts and also that this means beginning with rounded-off percentages such as 10%, 20% and 25%, which makes it easy to establish a direct relationship with fractions. Indeed, it appears logical to wait to introduce percentages such as 13% and 64% until later on. But there is also something odd in this approach; if percentages are only another way of writing down simple fractions, why were they ever invented? A store could just as easily write its advertisements as follows: "This week, you'll pay one-fourth less at our store", or "All DVD players at one-fifth discount." Percentages derive their right to exist from the limitations of regular fractions: fractions are difficult to compare with each other, and the scale that they provide is rather unrefined.

Two approaches are possible when introducing percentages. The first approach is to introduce percentages as a new way of writing down part-whole relationships, in addition to the fractional notation that the students already know. During this process, the usefulness of percentage notation is not addressed directly. The second approach is to introduce percentages as an invention, as the answer to a problem. We essentially allow the students to make the step to percentages themselves.

The introduction using the second approach begins with a discussion about the limitations of regular fractions. Present children with a situation in which comparing fractions makes things obscure, for example the problem about staying at school for lunch on page 92. In the discussion about the problem, it will emerge that you can use fractions to compare schools, but that they would end up being different fractions. The conclusion could then be that it is easier to work with a single type of fraction instead of with all kinds of different fractions. It will also probably emerge that "hundredths" offer a more refined scale than other types of fractions.

In the second approach, working with fractions is initially expanded to hundredths, and the children explore the advantages and disadvantages of using hundredths compared to regular fractions. The percentage notation is then introduced as an easier form of notation using these special hundredth fractions. This approach essentially offers students the possibility to discover the idea of percentages themselves. The second approach is advantageous because the students essentially make the step to percentages themselves, instead of this concept being introduced from the outside.

Both approaches are possible, but with the first approach an important question is: when will the discussion take place about the advantages and disadvantages of fractions with respect to percentages? After all, it would not be such a good thing if the children simply accepted the difference between fractions and percentages as a oddity of our arithmetic system.

Staying over at school

The municipality commissioned a study into how many children stay over for lunch at various schools.

Green Meadows School:	40 of 400
The Sundial:	210 of 350
River Amstel School:	210 of 240
Queen Beatrix:	300 of 400
The Fountain:	120 of 160
Huygens School:	90 of 270

Which school has a relatively large number of students who stay over for lunch, which school has relatively few? Because there are large differences in the numbers of students, the schools are difficult to compare. A possible solution is to convert the numbers into fractions, for example with the computer programme "Breukenstrook" ("Fraction bar" - www.rekenweb.nl). In this program, you enter the total numbers and find which fraction fits the best.

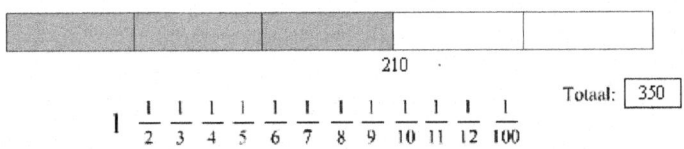

However, the resulting row of fractions is also difficult to compare: fifths, eighths, fourths, thirds; what can you do about this?

The discussion resulting from this problem can lead to the conclusion that in this situation it is useful to use the same type of fraction. In that case, for example, you could use eighths: Amstel $\frac{7}{8}$, Sundial $\frac{5}{8}$, etc., but you could also work with tenths and with hundredths. The discussion does not have to lead directly to working with hundredths as long as it is clear that it is much easier to compare things if they are expressed with the same type of fraction.

Models

The percentage bar

The most important model for percentages is the bar. The percentages are written above the bar and the corresponding numbers below the bar, or the other way around. The advantage of the bar is that it has "body" - area. For children, this makes it easier to talk in terms of "the whole" and "the so-much part" of the whole.

Compared with the bar, the double number line is a much more abstract model. On the other hand, the double number line is more logical when it concerns percentages above 100, because with this model it is self-evident that you can continue the line beyond 100%.

The percentage bar supports flexible mental arithmetic with percentages. For example, consider the question: "82% of 540 litres, how many litres is that?" Various lines of reasoning can be used to determine that the result must be more than 400 litres:

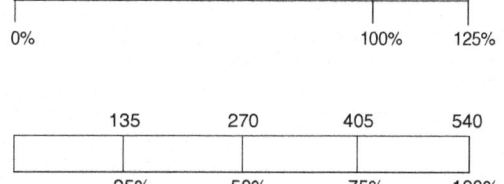

— half of 540 is 270, one-fourth is 135, therefore 75% is 405.
— 10% is 54, therefore 20% is 108 and 80% is 432.

In a learning-teaching trajectory for percentages, the emphasis should lie on flexible mental arithmetic. While engaging in this process, students can then discover that there is a method that always works - an algorithm - which involves first calculating how much 1% of something is. However, students then also discover that figuring via 1% is not always the easiest way. On the other hand, the 1% rule is extremely important when doing arithmetic on the calculator. We will return to this aspect later on in this chapter.

The percentage table

Besides the bar, the ratio table can also be used as an arithmetic aid. The calculation method that corresponds with the first bar above can then be written as follows:

Computer programs about percentages

A computer program that can help establish the relationship between fractions and percentages is "In Kaart" ("Circle diagrams and bars"). This program draws circle diagrams and bars when data are entered. Clicking on one of the fractions symbols below causes the circle diagram to be divided into the number of pieces that corresponds with that fraction. There is also a possibility to divide into hundredths. With the program, students can look for a compatible description in terms of percentages or fractions.

One of the exercises with the program is to have students ask in their own class what the other children prefer to do after school and to compare the results with those from a given study.

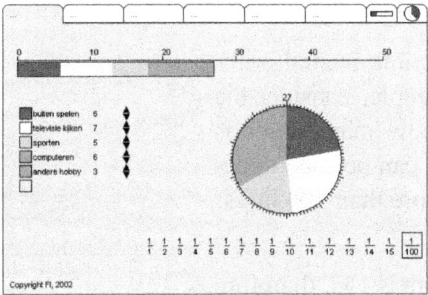

Another program is the percentage bar of "Rekenen met Stroken" ("Calculating with Bars"). The students can fill in a total themselves. Clicking on the bar then shows which numbers correspond with a specific part of the bar. The computer can also subdivide the bar into equal pieces, so that percentages and fractions can be compared. A series of example exercises is included with the program.

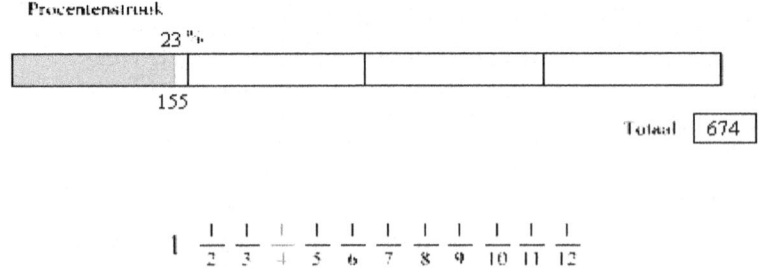

The computer programs can be found at www.rekenweb.nl.

94

100%	50%	25%	75%
540	270	135	405

As with the bar and the double number line, the percentage table offers the possibility to link numbers and percentages together, and like the bar and the double number line, the table offers the freedom to make all kinds of interim steps. One difference, however, is that in the table the numbers can be placed in random order. The disadvantage here is that it gives the calculation a more abstract quality, without the support of the bar for "so-much part of the whole"- reasoning.

The table and the bar can work well together. If you want to choose only one of the two for a standard aid, then you should choose the bar.

Calculating with percentages

Converting to fractions

It is important that students can convert percentages into fractions and the reverse. They must be able to do that because percentages and fractions are often used interchangeably in daily life; instead of "72%", someone might say "nearly three-fourths". It is also important because the process of converting the percentage into a regular fraction makes students familiar with the order of magnitude of percentages and therefore contributes to their numerical insight. This not only involves the fact that children are able to understand the "conversion" of 25% and 75%, but they must also be able to interpret percentages such as "64%" as "more than half, but less than $\frac{2}{3}$".

The relationship with fractions must be established by means of reasoning. The bar plays a major role in this process. By drawing, children learn that 25% is half of 50%, and therefore equal to one-fourth of 100%.

It is not necessary for children to have ready knowledge that 80% is equal to $\frac{4}{5}$, but they must be able to figure out that this is correct by making a drawing.

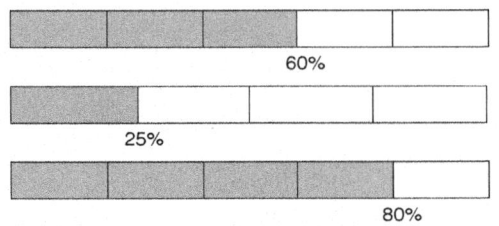

60%

25%

80%

Ultimately, students must have ready knowledge of relationships such as "25% is the same as $\frac{1}{4}$" and "$\frac{1}{3}$ is the same as $33\frac{1}{3}\%$". They develop this ready knowledge by reasoning with percentages and fractions. Memorizing the relationships as separate facts does not serve any real purpose.

23% of 674

In education, we tend to work with simplified numbers so that the arithmetic for the students is not too difficult. Exercises concerning percentages therefore often involve percentages such as 20%, 25%, 60%, and 75%, but almost never percentages such as 23% or 79%. The exercises almost always involve rounded numbers, usually numbers under 100. Exercises therefore tend to concern percentages such as "25% of 80", rather than "23% of 674". Although such simplifications are well intended, in one respect they negate the essence of what percentages have to offer, because percentages actually help us to understand proportions with large or difficult numbers. A proportion such as "155 of 674" is not easy for us to imagine. With numbers under 100, there is less need for percentages, because a proportion such as "17 of 84" does mean something to us. Moreover, if the numbers are even easier, such as "20 of 80", we can use regular fractions. We don't mean to say here that problems such as "20 of 80 is... %" should be avoided, quite the contrary. But there should also be attention for doing arithmetic with large numbers which aren't nicely rounded. This can only happen when students are allowed to make an estimation or if the real figuring is left to the computer or calculator.

Estimating with large numbers that aren't nicely rounded must be given a great deal of attention as part of a learning-teaching trajectory for percentages. In daily life, estimation plays a more important role than exact arithmetic. Moreover, children develop a feeling for numbers through estimation.

Percentages on the calculator

Students must be able to solve percentage problems using their numerical knowledge (network of relationships) and the bar as a model. With somewhat more difficult numbers, they must be able to estimate. Nevertheless, it is also important that students at a certain point learn to solve percentage problems with the calculator. After all, in daily life there is often a need for an exact result.

Many calculators have a percentage button, but the way this button works is not always immediately obvious. If you only occasionally have to calculate a percentage, it is easier to use the standard buttons for dividing and multiplying.
The 1% rule, which we previously described as being too rigid for mental arithmetic, plays an important role when working out problems on the calculator.
When using the calculator, it seems obvious to perform percentage calculations in the fewest possible number of steps. This stands in contrast to performing calculations using the ratio table, because in that case you can choose to take extra interim steps which simplify the calculating work. Doing arithmetic on the calculator therefore amounts to applying standard procedures. It is important that students use these procedures insightfully.

Figuring a part
How much is 12% of € 750? Such a question can be answered by first figuring out how much 1% of this amount is. Then that amount is multiplied by the percentage.

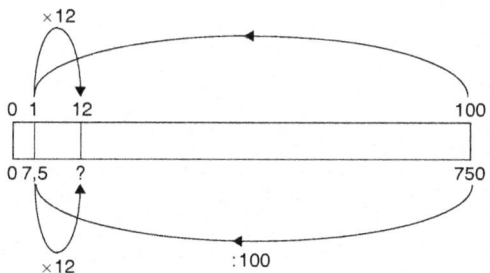

You first divide the whole by 100 and then multiply the result by the given percentage. This means that the following steps are carried out sequentially.

whole $:100$ → $\times$ percentage   →   part

We can also show the steps in a ratio table. We calculate the problem "what is 12% of € 750?" as follows:

100%	1%	12%
€ 750.00	€ 7.50	€ 90.00

When students understand that a percentage can be understood as a factor, the two steps can be combined into a single operation: multiplying by the decimal equivalent of the percentage:

whole $\times$ factor   →   part

We will address the topic of the percentage as a factor later on in this chapter.

Figuring the percentage

In order to convert the proportion between the part and the whole into a percentage, the interim step of 1% can be used. Consider the following example:

> "At the Sunnyside School, 60 of the 150 parents are opposed to the plans of the school administration. What percentage of the parents are opposed?"

This is shown with the bar below.

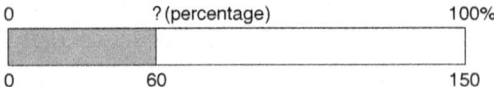

You can use the following reasoning: there are 150 parents, 1% of this number is 1.5. In order to know how much 60 of 150 is in percent, you must know how often 1.5 goes into 60. In "arrow language" this is shown as follows:

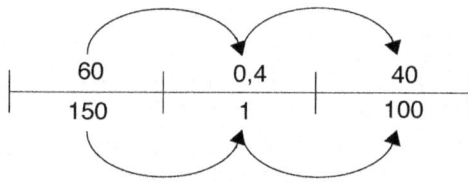

part ——————————→ percentage
        : (1% of the whole)

However, many adults do this differently. They divide the given amount by the total and multiply the result by 100.

————————→ ————————→ percentage
    : whole   × 100

As shown in a ratio table:

60	0,4	40
150	1	100

The fact that this procedure leads to the same result is not difficult to understand. In the first case you divide by a number that is a hundred times as small, and in the second case you multiply afterwards by 100. But this is reasoning at a formal level. A difficult aspect of the second method is how you should interpret the result of the interim step: what is this "0.4 of 1"? The answer to this question is that you first "standardize" to 1 and after that to 100. However, this also involves reasoning at a very formal level.

Because the first procedure is easier for students to understand, it is a good idea to emphasize this method for working out problems. But we can also make the second procedure available. After all, students develop a network of relationships from which they can reason that the second procedure also leads to the correct result. In this way they understand at a certain point that the ratio "3 to 4" fits with $3 : 4 = 0.75$ on the calculator and that in turn $\frac{3}{4} = 0.75$ is the same as 75%. And they know that "1:2", "20:40" and "80:160" all give the result of 0.5 on the calculator, which confirms that "$\frac{1}{2} = 0.5$" is the same as 50%. From these types of experiences, they can make the step to where they understand that proportions such as 60 to 150 or 63 to 155

Reduce to 80%

Enlarging and reducing on a photocopy machine provides an opportunity to study how a percentage can function as a multiplication factor. A few examples of questions are included below.

Is it true that an 80% reduction makes the lengths in the original 80% shorter? How can you check this?

- Make a copy of an arbitrary page and compare the lengths on the original and the copy. Multiplying the length in the original by 0.8 should provide the length on the copy.
- You can also choose an "easy" length beforehand. For example, place a 10 cm line on a sheet. On the reduced copy, the line should be 8 cm long.

It becomes more difficult when matters are reversed. One of the students makes a copy and chooses the amount of enlargement or reduction himself. Can the other students figure out the percentage of enlargement or reduction?

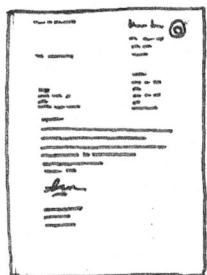 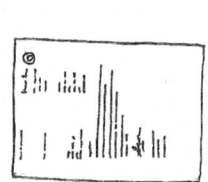

If you fold an A4 sheet in half, you get a format that is called "A5". How can you reduce an A4 to an A5 format on the photocopy machine? It turns out that you have to reduce it by 70%, and not by 50%, as many children initially think. The area of an A5 sheet is indeed half that of an A4 sheet, but the percentage reduction concerns length and width, not area.

Is the reduction exactly 70%? How can you use the calculator to find the exact number?

- A 10 cm x 10 cm square - therefore with an area of 100 cm^2 – should have an area of 50 cm^2 on an A5 copy. But if the copy machine is set to 70% reduction, the area becomes 49 cm^2 (7×7). Reducing by 71% results in an area of 50.41 cm^2 ($7,1 \times 7,1$) and that is again too big. The correct number is therefore somewhere between 70% and 71%.
- You can calculate the exact number on the calculator using square roots. The square root of 50 is 7.0710678. The reduction that you need therefore lies closer to 71% than 70%.

can lead to a decimal number that you can interpret as "so much with respect to 1".

Figuring the whole

> "You buy shoes and get a € 35 discount. That is a discount of 15%. How much do the shoes cost without the discount?"

For the sake of completeness, we have also included this type of exercise, although the problem is somewhat artificial. The part is known and you have to provide the whole. You can also answer this question by first calculating how much 1% is.

The part is first divided by the percentage, and then the result is multiplied by 100. The steps are shown below:

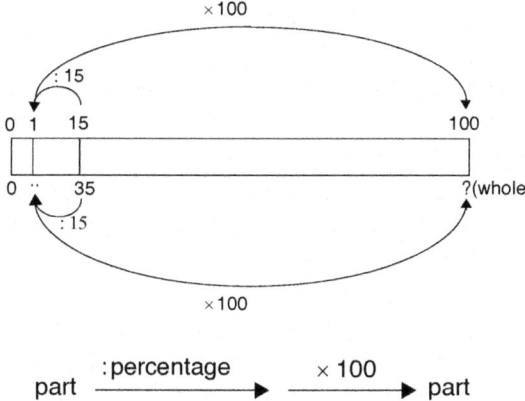

Percentage as a factor

A discount problem:

> "During a sale, you get a 15% discount on an MP3 player which originally cost € 82. How much will you have to pay?"

This problem can be figured in several steps, or more directly.

— In two steps: 1% is € 0.82, so 15% is 15 × 0,82; you will pay € 82,00 - € 12,30, therefore € 69,70.
— Start directly with the remaining percentage: 85 × 0,82 = € 69.70.

However, percentages can also be understood as a multiplication factor -

instead of "so many hundredths of". In that case we convert the percentage to a decimal. On the calculator this appears as follows:

- You can calculate 15% of 82 by multiplying 82 by 0.15.
- You can calculate the price of the MP3 player with 15% discount as 0.85×82.

The fact that this method of calculation provides the same result is not difficult to understand - $85 \times$ € 0.82 compared to $0.85 \times$ € 82 - but conceptually there is a major difference. In the first case, we make the step via 1%, where the multiplication - so many times 1% - can be interpreted as repeated addition. In the second case, we view the percentage as a multiplication factor. The latter assumes a relatively abstract, formal way of looking at percentages. For most children in primary school, this is asking too much, but the better mathematics students can make this step.

Enlargement and reduction on the photocopy machine provide a good opportunity to discuss the role of percentages as a factor. Enlargement and reduction cannot be interpreted as repeated addition or subtraction, because you can't add a piece so many times or subtract one so many times. It is better to say that every length in the original drawing changes in the same way - with the same multiplication factor. The box on page 127 shows examples of questions concerning enlargement and reduction on a photocopy machine.

Another way to bring up working with a percentage as a factor is to investigate what the calculator does. From "fair sharing", the students know that division problems such as 3 : 4 lead to the result $\frac{3}{4}$; the opposite reasoning, $\frac{3}{4}$ = 3 : 4, provides a way to enter fractions into the calculator by typing in 3 : 4. With this knowledge, students can now investigate how you can calculate 75% of 350 on the calculator.

During this process, the following arguments are used:

- 75% of 350 is $\frac{75}{100}$ of 350. You can find the $\frac{1}{100}$ part via 350 : 100 = 3.5. Then the $\frac{75}{100}$ part is 75 times as much, therefore $75 \times 3,5 = 262,5$.
- 75% is $\frac{3}{4}$, and $\frac{3}{4}$ is 0.75 on the calculator. Could you then multiply 0.75 times 350? Doing this operation on the calculator shows that you also get 262.5.

By comparing the various solutions, the students are going to see that the following calculations amount to the same thing:

$$350 \xrightarrow{\;:100\;} \xrightarrow{\;\times 75\;} 262.5$$

$$350 \xrightarrow{\;\times 75\;} \xrightarrow{\;:100\;} 262.5$$

$$350 \xrightarrow{\;\times 0.75\;} 262.5$$

The global learning-teaching trajectory

Percentages are introduced as a standardization of the description of part-whole relationships with fractions. At the beginning, students must therefore already have acquired the necessary elemental knowledge about fractions. Moreover, percentages are linked to "hundredths", which means that the students must be specifically familiar with these fractions. It is therefore an obvious step to begin percentages only after decimals have been addressed, at least the "common decimal fractions".

Introduction

Percentages are introduced as a handy way to compare part-whole relationships and proportions. The first activities with percentages therefore concern the conversion of part-whole relationships or proportions into percentages. After this, the percentage bar is developed as the primary model for percentages. This is first introduced as an aid for comparison and to support reasoning concerning the order of magnitude.

After the percentage bar has been introduced as a means to illustrate percentages, it is also used as a calculation aid. For example, proportions such as "72 of € 120" can be converted into a percentage in a series of steps:

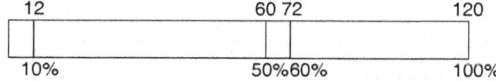

We begin by taking half of the total: € 120 is 100%, therefore € 60 is 50%. It must be slightly more than this. 10% of 120 is 12, so 60% is 72.

When 72 is recognized as 6 × 12, this process can be speeded up; € 12 is 10%, therefore € 72 is 60%.

Taking percentages

An important subsidiary objective of this type of activity is the development of numerical relationships that describe the correlations between fractions and percentages. These numerical relationships can then be used when "taking percentages". For example, 17% of 360 can be approached in an iterative fashion by using numerical relationships (such as the fact that $\frac{1}{3}$ is equal to $33\frac{1}{3}$%), which are illustrated on a bar.

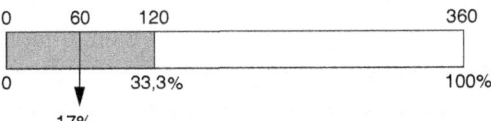

This reasoning can, of course, also be described with a ratio table.

percentage	100%	33.3%	16.6%
amount	360	120	60

Using the ratio table for taking percentages can be seen as a subsequent step. Essentially, you describe how you reason with the bar. As shown in the example, working in an iterative fashion is compatible with estimation, "60 is approximately 17% of 360". For exact calculation, we can work with the 1% method. However, estimation is an essential part of taking percentages, certainly in combination with establishing relationships with fractions.

In addition, there must also be attention to the comparison of and reasoning with proportions and relationships described with percentages. During this process, it is always important that the students realize what the percentage refers to.

During this phase, exercises are also provided concerning adding and subtracting percentages. When this leads to the amount of 100% being exceeded, you can switch to using the double number line.

Two types of ratio tables

When calculating with ratio tables, there must be explicit attention to the distinction between ratio tables that describe part-whole relationships, in which the percentage appears as "so many per 100" and ratio tables in which one of the number rows provides percentages. In the latter case, the question "what percentage is 36 of € 120?" could be answered as follows:

percentage	100%	10%	30%
amount	120	12	36

The ratio table with "so many per 100" could appear as follows:

part	36	3	30
whole	120	10	100

Doing arithmetic with the calculator

When students are sufficiently familiar with easy and flexible reasoning with percentages, using the calculator becomes a topic for investigation. This builds upon the insights that the students acquired when converting fractions into decimals on the calculator. For example, when calculating 15% of 82 by multiplying 15 times $\frac{1}{100}$ of 82 (on the calculator, 82 : 100 = 0.82; 15 × 0.82 = 12.3), which amounts to the same thing as $1\frac{15}{100}$ times 82 (on the calculator, 15 : 100 = 0.15; 0.15 × 82 = 12.3).

The curriculum continues based upon the insights that the students acquired when simplifying proportions, which can be associated with decimals via the corresponding division sum. For example, "789 of 5690" can be associated with the division sum 789 : 5690, which results in 0.138664 on the calculator, therefore approximately 0.14. This can then be interpreted as 14% (789 of 5690 is equivalent to 14 of 100, therefore, 789 is 14% of 5690).

More complex reasoning with factors can be used to explore this material in greater depth. For example a "25% discount" is equivalent to "0.75 × the price" and "plus 17.5% sales tax" means "multiplying by a factor of 1.175".

6 Core insights into decimals

Understanding decimals involves the central idea of systematic refinement with a factor of ten. In this context, it is important that the decimals are properly embedded in reasoning with "regular tenth fractions" and working with measurements from the metric system. An important support pillar for calculating with decimals is the idea of shifting the measurement scales; by taking a "detour" through another scale of measurement, you can calculate with whole numbers. Sometimes simple fractions can offer a solution, certainly when the numbers are transformed in such a way that you can make an estimation with "easy numbers". On the other hand, fractions, proportions and percentages must be converted into decimals whenever the calculator is used. A difficult issue is understanding that this involves a form of multiplication with "part of" relationships.

Refining number

Knowing the rule does not mean that you understand the process

Children become acquainted with decimals when they are very young. They learn that € 2.45 stands for 2 euros and 45 cents, they see decimals on the produce scale at the supermarket, soft drink bottles state their contents as 0.7 or 1.5 litre, and they perhaps know that their height can be not only written down as 1 metre and 54 cm but also as 1.54 m. Within such fixed contexts, however, decimals for children are nothing more than numbers that can be written in a special way. They do not understand that the figures to the right of the decimal point ensure a more precise description, neither do they realize that we can theoretically continue adding more decimals indefinitely. In the same way that it is a major discovery for young children to learn that there is no "biggest number", it will also be exciting for them to learn that there is no limit to the number of possible decimals to the right of the decimal point.

Monetary amounts are probably the decimals that children encounter most frequently, but money is actually not a very good context with respect to the structure of decimals. Students calculate with money by interpreting the figures to the left and the right of the decimal point as independent numbers. They read € 2.45 as "2 euros and 45 cents", where the euros and cents are separate amounts, linked with each other via an exchange rule. Many aspects of decimals are not encountered when working with money. We write prices with euros and cents (€ 2.45), or in whole euros (€ 399 or € 399.00), but we never write monetary amounts by leaving off the zero at the end (€ 2.4 instead of € 2.40), which we certainly do with other decimal numbers. Moreover, there are never more than two decimals to the right of the decimal point. Children don't usually encounter exchange rates, where $ 1.00 may be equivalent to € 0.773973, for example. In short, the fact that children encounter decimals so frequently in daily life does not automatically mean that they perceive the underlying system.

Insight into structure

Students often have a great deal of difficulty with decimals. This is apparent, for example, when we ask them whether 1.65 is larger or smaller than 1.9. Many children will choose 1.65, because 65 is larger than 9, isn't it? What makes decimals so difficult is that we usually leave off the zeros at the end. Even the calculator does this; if you enter 15.34 + 2.05, the calculator gives the answer as 17.39, but it gives 17.4 as the answer to 15.34 + 2.06. The result is that we often have to compare figures that have varying numbers of decimals to the right of the decimal point.

Whether or not it is correct to leave off the zeros is still a matter for discussion; for example, physicists insist that 3.400 is a completely different measurement result than 3.4. If you measure length with varying degrees of precision, a result of 3.4 m should mean that the actual length lies between 3.35 m and 3.45 m, while 3.400 m means that it lies between 3.3995 m and 3.4005 m. In the latter case, the precision is 1 millimetre.

For many children, calculating with decimals is a terrain full of mysterious rules. Consider the procedures for adding or subtracting decimals. Do students understand why they have to align the decimal points directly under each other, even when there are differing numbers of decimals to the right of the decimal point? Or is that only a memorized rule for them? The procedure for working out a multiplication problem with decimals is even more difficult to understand. As with fractions, this lack of understanding will not be alleviated by having the students practice more. It is much more important that the students develop insight into the structure of decimals. What also makes decimals difficult is that we refer to decimals with the terms "tenths" and "hundredths", but these tenths and hundredths do not appear at all similar to the fractions with which the children are familiar. The solution to this problem, as we will discuss later on, is that we must make it clear to the children why they are called tenths and hundredths. We can do this in several ways, for example by placing the decimal notation explicitly alongside the notation with fractions. The link with fractions helps students understand the structure of decimals.

Decimal refinement

For us it is self-evident that a metre can be divided into 10 decimetres, a decimetre into 10 centimetres, a centimetre into 10 millimetres, and so forth. However, considering how long people worked with measurements such as yards, feet and inches, it is clear that our metric system of measurement is not at all self-evident. That system is based on three basic principles:

– Every step in increasing precision uses the same type of refinement.
– The refinement proceeds in steps of 10.
– There are no limits to the refinement.

The system also works in the other direction. "Decametres" and "hectometres" are measurements that we do not frequently use in daily life, but we do use "kilometres".

The implementation of the metric system of measurement, which took place under the administration of Napoleon, was a radical break with the past; in the old measurement systems the refinements did not proceed in steps of 10, and every step was different from the preceding one. For example, an "Amsterdam foot" contained 3 "palms", and each palm contained four "thumbs", so a foot was 12 thumbs. With volume measurements, refinement by repeated halves was common: whole, half, fourth, eighth. This tendency is still apparent today, as shown by the fact that cream is sold in containers of $\frac{1}{8}$ litre, even though this is indicated on the package with "125 cl".

Around 1600, there was a movement towards working with decimals or decimal fractions. The Dutch author Simon Stevin explained the system in a book called De Thiende. The advantage of tenth fractions or decimals - the above author did not yet write them with a decimal point - is that you can calculate with them as if they were regular numbers. It is a beautiful, elegant system that continues the decimal structure of the whole numbers - ones, tens, hundreds and so on - to the other side of the decimal point. In 1795, Napoleon introduced the metric system in the Netherlands for weights and measurements, but it took a long time before it became widely used, and we still encounter remainders of other measurement systems.

The introduction of decimals

A tenth of a tenth

A fairly customary way of introducing decimals is to begin by discussing what students already know about them. Children are familiar with decimals in the context of money and measurements of length and volume. The risk of such an approach, however, is that the teacher quickly gains the impression that the students understand everything. It is only when we present them with a new situation that it becomes clear that their understanding of the decimal system still has many gaps.

Because the topics of measurement, the metric system and decimals are closely related, we can introduce decimals from measurement problems. One possible approach is sketched out in the lesson series "A tenth of a tenth", see the text box on pages 112 and 113. In the lesson series, children are presented with the problem of what you can do when you have to measure with a string or a bar that is too large to make a precise measurement. When testing the lesson series in a class from grade 5, it turned out that it was immediately obvious for all children that they could divide the bar into smaller pieces, for example by drawing marks on the bar. After this there was a discussion about what a useful subdivision system would be. What is the best number of subdivisions for the bar? All kinds of arguments emerged in favour of a subdivision into six pieces, or eight or ten. The subdivision into 10 pieces did not win the debate on its own merits - when testing the lessons, this was ultimately suggested by the teacher as a standard - but it became clear through the discussions that it is useful to have a system of refinement, and that such a system should offer the possibility to make increasingly precise measurements.

A distinctive feature of this introduction to decimals is that during the first lessons the students work with regular tenth fractions. For example, students write down their measurement data as: "2 bars plus $\frac{7}{10}$ bar". And if they are investigating the relationship with metres and centimetres, they initially write: "40 cm = $\frac{4}{10}$ m" and "95 cm = $\frac{95}{100}$ m". The teacher introduces decimal point notation only after a number of lessons. This has the advantage of establishing a very explicit relationship between fractions and decimals.

Continually return to the meaning

The approach that we sketch out in the lesson series "A tenth of a tenth" is certainly not the only way to introduce decimals. In any case, the introduction is only a small part of the whole story. It is important that the teacher constantly keeps asking questions about the structure of decimals. The following list provides some examples of questions that should regularly be addressed:

– What is the relationship between 1.6 and 1.65?
– Why do we sometimes write 1.60 and don't always leave the zeros off at the end?
– Why does the calculator tell us that $\frac{1}{4}$ is equal to 0.25, but for $\frac{1}{3}$ it gives us a strange number like 0.333333?
– Does it matter if you enter 3.8 instead of 3.80 on the calculator, or 5.00 instead of 5? In which ways can you enter 24 × € 0.70? Can you explain why you get the same result?
– Do numbers exist such as 0.0002, and what do they mean if they do exist? Is 0.0002 larger or smaller than zero?
– What happens if you multiply 0.04 by 10? What does it mean if you shift the decimal point one position, to the right or to the left?

Calculating with decimals

Estimation or exact calculation

When calculating with decimals, a distinction must be made between men-

Lessonseries "A tenth of a tenth"

The lesson series "A tenth of a tenth" can be used to introduce decimals, but it can also be used in grade 6 as a review of the system of decimals.[1] Below we will describe the experiences in a class in grade 5, where the lesson series was used as an introduction.

The teacher begins the first lesson with a story about her sister who has a farm, and from there goes to the question of how people formerly measured land area. There was a time when people did not use metres, centimetres and kilometres; how would they have indicated how big a field was? One of the students suggests measuring the sides of the field by repeatedly using a length of wire. There is a discussion about how this would take place in practice.

The teacher then shows the students a piece of string - which is exactly one metre long, but she doesn't say this at the time - and asks the children to measure their tables with this string. Tables that are placed together appear to be nearly two times one length of string. Jeroen thinks that it is one string plus $\frac{4}{5}$ string. Tisse says that you can write that as "$1\frac{4}{5}$ string".

The teacher proposes putting marks on the string, because then you could use it to measure all kinds of things. She asks the class how you could best divide up such a string. There are many suggestions: in fourths, sixths, fifths, eights, tenths and twelfths. Some students are in favour of twelfths because you could make these into thirds and fourths. Fenne explains why she chose eight pieces; with eight pieces you can easily show whether it is perhaps one-half or one-fourth. But she says, you can also continue on to 16 pieces, if eight is not precise enough.

The teacher summarizes the discussion and says that she has heard some good arguments. In any case it is important that an agreement is made about a standard that everyone will use. She explains that at a certain time in the past, people decided on a subdivision into 10 pieces.

In a subsequent lesson, the students begin to measure small objects with a strip of paper that is $\frac{1}{10}$ the length of the string from the previous lesson. Once again, this brings up the discussion about the question of what would be a useful subdivision if you want to measure even more precisely. This discussion also ends with the observation that people in the past chose to make a further refinement by subdividing into tenths.

In the lesson after this, the link between metres and centimetres is established; the long string is 1 metre, the shorter strip is 10 centimetres. The shorter strip is then subdivided into 10 pieces, and the teacher asks about the relationship between the long string and such a very small piece. The students discover that a tenth of the small strip is $\frac{1}{100}$ metre.

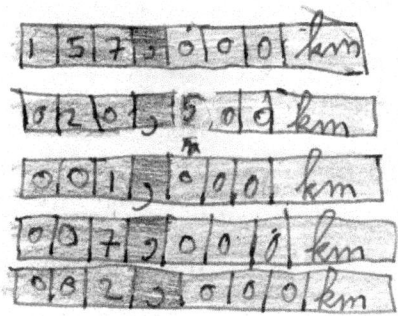

$$60\ cm \longrightarrow \frac{6}{10}$$

$$55\ cm \longrightarrow \frac{55}{100}$$

$$30\ cm \longrightarrow \frac{3}{10}$$

$$25\ cm \longrightarrow \frac{2,5}{10}$$

$$10\ cm \longrightarrow \frac{1}{10}$$

$$98\ cm \longrightarrow \frac{98}{100}$$

$$100\ cm \longrightarrow \frac{100}{100}$$

After this the students investigate how you can describe strips of 60 cm, 55 cm, 30 cm, 25 cm and so forth as "the fractional part of a metre". Strips of 60 cm and 30 cm do not cause any problems - they are obviously $\frac{6}{10}$ and $\frac{3}{10}$ of a metre - but the other sizes lead to discussion.

With the problem of the 25 cm length, Tisse formulates her answer as follows: it is $\frac{2}{10}$ and $\frac{1}{2}$ of a tenth. Other children use the $\frac{1}{20}$ fraction for half of $\frac{1}{10}$. Ruben chooses yet another notation. He believes you should write down this strip length as $\frac{2.5}{10}$.

Mathijs is one of the students who immediately makes the transition to one hundredths, and with the 25 cm length he comes up with $\frac{25}{100}$ strip. He explains how 10 pieces of one hundredth fit into $\frac{1}{10}$ strip.

During the following lesson, the teacher uses an earlier discussion about the odometer on a tractor to talk about how you can also write down these types of measurements with decimal points.

While testing this series of lessons, it was striking that students in the discussions did not come up with any arguments that they derived from their knowledge of measurement. They knew that the long strip given to them by the teacher was approximately a metre long - in fact it was exactly 1 m long - but they did not argue in favour of a subdivision of the long strip into 100 pieces, or for a subdivision into 10 and then 10 again. This appears to be strange, because how could they have forgotten that this in fact involves a strip one metre long? We interpret this

caption: odometres

as an indication that the students have apparently not understood the system underlying length measurements. They did know what decimetres, centimetres and millimetres are, but they had not yet realized that these measurements arc based on a system of continuous refinement with steps of 10. In any case, they apparently did not see the advantages of this system of measurement refinement, and in that regard the series of decimal lessons also contributed to their understanding about measurement.

tal arithmetic and doing calculations on the calculator. With mental arithmetic, it is a good idea to allow differentiation according to various levels of precision. In Chapter 1, we used the example of the price sticker for 0.762 kg of apples for € 1.20 per kilo; in Chapter 7 on differentiation we will return to this example. A comparable example is the following.

> Liesbeth purchases 1.6 m of cloth for a dress. The cloth costs € 12.50 per metre. Approximately how much will she have to pay?

The students are asked for an estimation. They might come up with answers such as:

– You need slightly more than $1 \frac{1}{2}$ metres. If the cloth costs € 12.00 per metre, half a metre would cost € 6.00. It would therefore cost slightly more than € 18.00.
– If the cloth costs € 12.00 per metre, 10 cm would cost € 1.20. A piece of cloth 60 cm long would cost € 7.20, and one 1.6 m long would cost € 19.20. But this cloth is somewhat more expensive, so you would have to pay about € 20.00.
– The problem involves the multiplication of 1.6×12.50. This is the same as 0.8×25 or 0.4×50 or 0.2×100, and the answer to all these is 20. You must therefore pay € 20.00.

The answers reflect the mathematics knowledge of students. For the first explanation, a student must see 1.6 as "slightly more than 1 metre and $\frac{1}{2}$ metre". In the second solution, the student changes measurement scales: 1.6 m is 160 cm, and therefore 16 pieces of 10 cm. The third solution does not involve the context at all, and the multiplication is figured by taking halves and doubling.

If we allow students to solve such a problem with varying degrees of precision, we must at the same time require that they can provide an exact answer using the calculator.

Numerical relationships

Calculating with decimals is also based on the repertoire of numerical relationships that the students have already acquired. At the time decimals are addressed, students should, for example know the following:

- $\frac{1}{5} = \frac{2}{10}$
- $4 \times 25 = 100$; $4 \times 2\frac{1}{2} = 10$

At this time, it is also useful if students have established a relatively extensive network of relationships concerning numbers such as 20, 25, 33 $\frac{1}{3}$ and 12 $\frac{1}{2}$. The known relationships must not remain limited to $5 \times 20 = 100$, $4 \times 25 = 100$, $3 \times 33\frac{1}{3} = 100$ (or 3×33 is approximately 100) and $8 \times 12\frac{1}{2} = 100$, but should also comprise relationships such as $3 \times 25 = 75$, $2 \times 33\frac{1}{3} = 66\frac{2}{3}$ (or $2 \times 33 = 66$). To this end, students must be fluent in calculating with simple fractions.

Addition and subtraction with decimals

The analogy between calculating with whole numbers and calculating with decimals makes calculating with decimals simpler in a number of ways than calculating with fractions. However, one precondition is that students must understand the structure of decimals. It is only after students understand the nature of decimals that the rule "align the decimal points vertically" becomes more than an arbitrary procedure. In practice, the calculator is almost always used when calculating with decimals, and therefore it is not necessary to have students practice extensively with working out problems by hand. The addition and subtraction sums that we have students solve without using the calculator should primarily focus on increasing their insight into the structure of decimals. As an example, we take the following sum.

$0.14 + 0.7 =$

With this sum, students initially tend to give 0.21 as the answer, because $14 + 7$ equals 21. Of course, we can teach students a rule - "first make the number of digits to the right of the decimal point equal by adding zeros" - but if that is only a trick to get the right answer, we do not really help them. A better approach is to explicitly establish the relationship with fractions. In that case, it concerns the addition of $\frac{14}{100} + \frac{7}{10}$. In order to complete this sum, you must also convert $\frac{7}{10}$ into hundredths.

Another possibility with similar sums is to have children think of the measurement context. If the problem concerned 0.14 litres + 0.7 litres, you could convert that to: 14 cl plus 7 dl, and that is the same as 14 cl + 70 cl. Or you could think of 0.14 m + 0.7 m, which is 14 cm + 70 cm. In this way students use their knowledge of measurement to give meaning to calculating with decimals.

When calculating with decimals takes place within a context, this context can repeatedly be used to give meaning to the operations. With "abstract sums" (without context), students can be taught to convert these into a more familiar measurement context. In addition, we believe that teachers should regularly establish the relationship with regular fraction notation. The terminology that is used is already that of regular fractions: "tenths", "hundredths", "thousandths". By occasionally using the notation with a fraction line, we encourage students to use their knowledge of fractions when calculating with decimals.

Multiplication with decimals

It is not easy for students to give meaning to abstract multiplication problems with decimals. A sum such as 5×0.132 does not cause many problems - they can see this problem as the repeated addition of 0.132. But if the numbers in the sum are reversed, what would 0.132×5 stand for? As with multiplication of fractions, it is confusing that the result of 0.132×5 is smaller than 5. Children associate multiplication very strongly with things becoming larger.

Calculating with decimals results in fewer problems if meaningful contexts are used, but then the students may not understand that this actually concerns multiplication. In Chapter 1, we described how we showed a price sticker to students from grades 5 and 6; the sticker showed 0.762 kg of apples priced at € 1.20 per kg. The students came up with useful estimates, but none of the students could think how you could use the calculator to solve such a problem. Apparently the students did not understand that the result concerned a multiplication sum: 1.20×0.762. The literature on this topic has shown that this type of problem occurs very frequently with multiplication using decimals.

One difference with fractions is that when calculating with decimals it is often possible to shift measurement scales, where the numbers can be converted into a more familiar form. Take the following situation as an example:

Cloth costs € 6.00 per metre. If a piece of cloth is 0.65 m long, how much does it cost? Various approaches are possible:

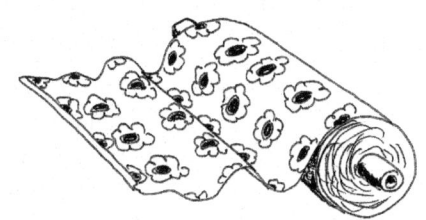

– We can eliminate the decimal points entirely by converting the length to 65 cm and the price to 600 cents per 100 cm, therefore 6 cents per cm. On the calculator, the price can be calculated as 65 × 6, therefore 390 cents.
– We can also enter 65 × 0.06, because six cents is € 0.06. On the calculator this gives the answer of 3.9, which must be read as € 3.90.
– We can take the length as the decimal - 0.65 m - and the price per metre. Entering 0.65 × 6 (or 0.65 × 6.00) gives the result that we had previously: 3.9.

By choosing different measurements - metres or centimetres, euros or cents - the result can be calculated in different ways. Of course, it is important that the students always realize with which measurement they are calculating.

The calculator is not only an aid to finding the result, but can also be used to investigate operations with decimals. What happens with the result of 1.5 × 7.4 if you make the first number 10 times as large? And what happens if you make both numbers 10 times as large? Can you explain why this happens? For some of the students, we will have to ask such questions within a context situation, such as the price of a piece of cloth. However, there are also students who can answer these types of questions outside the context. For them, decimals already have sufficient meaning in themselves.

Division with decimals

On the calculator, dividing two whole numbers often results in a decimal. Sharing money is a possible context to investigate this phenomenon. If four children are allowed to share 5 euros, every child gets € 1.25. This is exactly the same as the answer that appears on the calculator. It is interesting to see what happens when we choose other numbers.

– If four children share 8 euros, the calculator shows 8 : 4 = 2. They each get € 2.00.
– Sharing six euros results in an answer of 1.5 on the calculator, which

we can read as € 1.50. Perhaps we must briefly return to regular fractions: $\frac{5}{10}$ is the same as $\frac{50}{100}$.

- If eight children share 9 euros, the calculator gives the answer 1.125. This means that everyone can receive € 1.12 and then a few cents remain. Or if we round off to the closest 10 cents, then everyone gets € 1.10. The obvious question is: which amount can be divided evenly between nine children?
- If three children share 4 euros, the calculator gives the answer 1.3333333. Why is this? When would everyone get € 1.30? When would everyone get exactly € 1.33?

A useful follow-up assignment is to have the children individually search for division sums that result in one digit, two digits, three digits, etc. to the right of the decimal point.

The operations that children understand for whole numbers can be carried through in various ways to calculating with decimals.

- Measuring. With a problem such as 2 : 0.25, we can think of a situation such as: how often does 0.25 m go into 2 m? Or: how often does € 0.25 go into € 2.00? Within this context, it does not seem strange that the result is larger than the two with which we began, which never happens when you are dividing by a whole number.
- Viewing division as the reverse of multiplication. With a sum such as 2 : 0.25 we can look for the corresponding multiplication sum, therefore ... × 0.25 = 2. When we think of a context, this is comparable with measuring in steps.
- Seeking easier numbers. When dividing with whole numbers you can multiply or divide both numbers by the same amount. This can sometimes result in a sum which is easier to calculate, for example 105 : 15 = 210 : 30 (both numbers multiplied by 2) or 105 : 15 = 21 : 3 (both divided by 5). With a division problem you can therefore multiply numbers by 10 or 100 so that you get a number without a decimal point.

Focus on the calculator

From the examples discussed above, it appears that the calculator is a central focus when calculating with decimals. Spending time working out problems with decimals by hand is simply not very useful, if for no other reason than because all students have a calculator within easy reach from the first day of secondary education. There are various opinions about the calculator being so widely accepted in secondary education, but that does not mean that using it for calculation involves nothing more than entering numbers. Quite the contrary, the examples in this chapter have shown that students in fact must understand a great deal about decimals in order to use the calculator correctly.

A global learning-teaching trajectory

Numerical relationships

Numerical relationships concerning divisors of 100 and 1000 (such as 20, 25, 125 and 250) establish a foundation for handy and insightful calculation with decimals. These numerical relationships can also be addressed as part of measurement, in the form of part/whole relationships. For example, this concerns relationships such as "three-fourths of a kilometre is 750 metres", or "one-eighth litre cream is 125 ml".

"Common decimal fractions"

Decimals are essentially "simple decimal fractions" that are written in a specific way. We therefore believe that the basis for learning decimals is established by calculating with simple fractions having the denominators 10, 100 and 1000. In accordance with the structure sketched out at the end of Chapter 4, the relationships between fractions having the denominators 10, 100 and 1000 are investigated in the context of systematic refinement. This is described, for example, in the lesson series "A tenth of a tenth". Preceding this phase, the relationships between tenths and hundredths do not yet have to be addressed extensively, but it is important that the students have a well-established picture of fractions, so that the meaning of "simple" decimal fractions is clear for them.

Alternatively, teachers can choose to capitalize on the knowledge that students already have due to their experience with decimals in the contexts of money and length measurement, where the various units in the metric system (such as decimetres, centimetres, millimetres etc.) are used to give meaning to the figures to the right of the decimal point. We will not go any further with this alternative here.

The curriculum then focuses on developing relationships surrounding simple decimal fractions. Besides addition and subtraction - where you can convert tenths into hundredths and possibly into thousandths if necessary - it also comprises different ways of understanding a single number. For example, students must be able to see $2\frac{38}{100}$ as $2 + \frac{3}{10} + \frac{8}{100}$, but also as $\frac{238}{100}$. In addition, the students also begin to describe the relationships between tenths, hundredths and thousandths in terms of elementary multiplication and division sums such as $\frac{1}{10} \times \frac{1}{10} = \frac{1}{100}$, $10 \times \frac{1}{100} = \frac{1}{10}$ and $\frac{1}{100} : 10 = \frac{1}{1000}$.

Decimal notation and calculating with decimals

It is only when the students become familiar with calculating using tenths, hundredths and thousandths that decimal notation is introduced. Or perhaps it is better to say that the notation is explained, because students are already familiar with decimal notation as used in "money calculation" and measuring. The step that must be made here is from seeing "numbers to the left and the right of the decimal point as two different types of numbers, for which there is an exchange rule", to seeing "decimals as a representation of a system of denominators with increasing powers of 10".

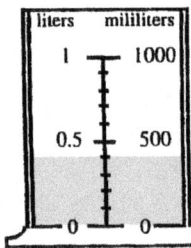

In this phase, the network of relationship has also expanded with relationships involving common fractions, such as $0.5 = \frac{1}{2}$, $0.25 = \frac{1}{4}$, $0.75 = \frac{3}{4}$, $0.2 = \frac{1}{5}$, $0.125 = \frac{1}{8}$. Here as well, the support offered by measurement and money calculation can be used.

After this, when calculating with decimals a relatively long time is spent on explicitly using the meaning of fractions or shifting scales of measurement. In order to prevent the students from starting to work with decimals by learning tricks, the operations are temporarily described in terms of "common decimal fractions" or as labelled fractions.

When the meaning of decimals is well understood, addition and subtraction will not be a problem. The same applies to multiplication and division sums that can be understood as repeated addition or repeated subtraction. Multiplication sums in contexts that can be understood as "part of" - as we have previously seen - can be solved at various levels. For this purpose, the students do not have to realize that it concerns multiplication; in estimation, it is sometimes the informal meaning that is used.

At the same time, the relationship between "taking part of something" and "multiplication" is regularly addressed. Working with the calculator is also involved in this phase. Besides using the calculator in situations where different scales of measurement play a role, more formal reasoning is also investigated. For example, $\frac{457}{1000}$ of an amount is determined by first finding the 1000th part of that amount on the calculator and then multiplying the results by 457. This is done in order to compare "457 divided by 1000" times that amount. For division, a similar line is followed as that for multiplication.

Doing sums on the calculator

To supplement estimation and exact calculation by hand, the students also learn to use the calculator. They begin with simple calculations. Later on, doing sums with decimals on the calculator is also used for many applications, such as converting fractions and proportions into decimals by means of division. During this process, for example, the proportion "3 of 8" becomes associated with $\frac{3}{8}$, which is again understood as the result of 3 divided by 8, which results in 0.375 on the calculator. During this process, the students must also learn to deal with the results of division problems that do not have a "nice" result, such as "3 : 7". Finally, this process of working with decimals on the calculator also includes calculating with percentages.

7 Differentiation

Introduction

In grades 3 through 6 of primary school, there are large differences between the students; when teaching difficult parts of the curriculum such as fractions, percentages, decimals and proportions, teachers will be continuously confronted with these differences. They are faced with the complex task of taking account of these differences in order to provide an adequate education not only for the slower students, but also for the better ones in the class. We can deal with this differentiation in many ways. We see that many teachers and teams choose to work with groups at various levels. The most far-reaching form of this approach is "streaming", where the class is divided into three or more groups, each of which works on their own mathematics topics and receives separate instruction. We believe this is not a sensible approach, especially because scheduling separate times for instruction means that the time the teacher has for instruction must be divided between different streams. As a result, the teacher lacks the time that is necessary to go into a single topic more deeply, and there will be a high probability that the instruction will go no further than explaining how you do the sum. The emphasis then lies on practicing procedures instead of developing understanding.

A better way to realize differentiation during the mathematics lesson is by allowing all students to participate in class discussions, but then making a distinction during the individual work. Such a differentiation approach has a number of elements that we will address below.

Class discussions

Once per week, or no more than twice per week, there is a discussion with the entire class focusing on the development of insight. By class discussion we mean a real discussion, with a great deal of contribution from the students. The starting point will often be a somewhat more difficult mathematics problem, for which the approach is not yet clear. The teacher will first give students the time - preferably in groups - to look for a solution to the problem and after that to compare the solutions during the discussion. The mathematics problem is the reason why the children are verbally formulating their insight; this does not mean that the most efficient or the "best" approach must be found. The discussion that is elicited by the problem ensures that children sharpen their insights or develop new ideas. We believe that all students can participate in such class discussions, but that the discussion must focus on core ideas and not on arithmetic procedures.

Individual work

When working individually, the students do not all work on the same problems. For example, they all begin with the assignment that is related to the class discussion of that week, but the better students can then go to work individual on more complicated assignments. While the students are working individually, the teacher can work with a small group on specific aspects.

Doing mathematics at your own level

It is important that the students be given space to do mathematics in their own way, both in the class discussions and when working individually. For example, students who have difficulty with percentages should be allowed to figure percentage sums using the percentage bar. However, the better students quickly simplify the percentage bar to one with just a few numbers, or no longer require such a model at all. But the better students can still be expected to use such a model to explain their solutions. Later on in this chapter, we will discuss how we must also accept the fact that children come up with various types of results: one child will find the exact result, while another child will provide an estimate. The emphasis, as stated previously, must lie on the class discussions. Not so much in terms of lesson time - because a single lesson with an intensive class discussion per week still allows great deal of time for other activities - but in the sense that class discussions determine the development of the children. Individual work during the other lessons must be coordinated with the discussions.
The fact that we emphasize the class discussions emerges from the choice that we made previously to focus on understanding and reasoning instead of practicing arithmetic procedures.

In this context, we must reflect on how we define "instruction". Often, instruction amounts to holding a class discussion about a specific type of exercise, as an introduction to individually completing the exercise. However, this is much different than the class discussion that we referred to above. With this limited meaning of the concept of instruction in mind, we would argue in favour of less instruction and more class discussions. On many days, the instruction could perhaps remain limited to a brief explanation of what the students are going to do individually, while at the same time a substantial amount of time could be reserved once per week for discussion.

Such an approach differs from the approach in the textbooks currently used in the Netherlands. These call for a class discussion three or four times per week, but these discussions usually do not concern fundamental issues. In the prescribed methods, the curriculum is laid out in great detail with a carefully planned progression in the assignments, which enables the students to make a series of small, new steps. The downside of such an approach is that the students are not stimulated to see the big picture. In our view, it is important to hold regular discussions with students that go further than talking about the assignment at hand, for example by asking fundamental questions concerning the insights and the operations with which the students have meanwhile become familiar, or by presenting students with problems that are essentially a preview of the subject matter that will be coming later on.

The most important question called up by such an approach is the following: is it really possible to hold discussions with the entire class during which both the slower students and the better ones can learn something? We believe that this is indeed possible, but only if the teacher focuses on the conceptual core. In this chapter we will discuss what this means in practice and we will formulate a number of guidelines for such education.

Present open assignments

The assignment below was previously discussed in Chapter 2 and does not deviate very much from those that are used in the Dutch mathematics books for primary school. The difference is that these textbooks often state the type of solution that is expected.

> Candy for diabetics is expensive. It costs € 20 per kilo. These sweets are usually not sold by the kilo, but in smaller packages. There are packages of 125 g and 200 g. Figure out how much both packages cost.

In the standard method, for example, a ratio table will already be available. Indeed, figuring with the ratio table is one possible approach:

weight	1000 g	100 g	25 g	125 g
price	€ 20.00	€ 2.00	€ 0.50	€ 2.50

However, if the problem is presented in an open fashion, it turns out that the children also come up with other types of reasoning, such as a solution using fractions:

- 125 g is $\frac{1}{8}$ kg. You can divide € 20.00 by 8 and you have your answer right away.
- 200 g is $\frac{1}{5}$ kg. You can divide € 20.00 by 5.

Or students can use proportion reasoning, but they write it down differently:

1 kg costs € 20.00
100 g costs € 2.00
25 g costs € 0.50
125 g costs € 2.50

The above solutions essentially amount to the same thing, but the students experience them as totally different calculation methods. By having them compare their solutions, the differences and similarities become clear. Even more important is that the presentation of the problem in an open fashion stimulates the students to search for an approach themselves, instead of trying to follow a prescribed approach.

Offering an open problem would in this case essentially amount to the following:

- Leave out everything that steers the students towards a specific mathematics approach. For example, if there is a ratio table in the mathematics book, the teacher can introduce the problem on the blackboard, and have the students look at the book later on.
- Welcome all solutions or attempts at solutions from students, and investigate together with the students if you can arrive at the answer using the proposed solutions.
- Make it clear that different methods of working out a problem are almost always possible.

Class discussions based on the contribution of students

Class discussions almost always begin with a context problem. However, in the end it is not that specific problem which is important, but the ideas that the children develop by discussing such problems. Students must therefore be given plenty of space to verbalize their ideas.

Class discussions are the heart of mathematics education. Of course, practicing is also important, but learning in the sense of adapting one's ideas and making discoveries takes place primarily during class discussions. If it is going well, such a discussion takes place largely between the students themselves. However, the teacher plays a key role. She mediates, for example by reformulating the children's suggestions, and she ensures that the discussion concerns the points that she believes are important, but preferably using the ideas of the students as a point of departure.

However, there are major differences between the students. Is it actually possible to present the same problems to the entire class with such large differences? Don't some students immediately know the solution, while other students perhaps can't even follow the discussion about the solution? How can you as a teacher ensure that every child learns as much as possible from the mathematics problems that we present to the students?

In this section and the following one, we will attempt to formulate a number of guidelines for holding class discussions.

Present open assignments

A true context problem can always be solved in various ways. The teacher should allow this to resonate in the way in which she introduces the problem: the important thing is not to find the solution, but to figure out an approach to the solution yourself. An example of such an approach is shown on page 126.

This example shows that slower students can also find the answer to a question if we do not demand that they have to provide the exact answer. We therefore do not have to avoid problems with difficult numbers, but we should still offer students a safety net. Generally speaking, the best approach is to offer the problems in a very tangible context, so that the students can fall back on what they already know about similar situations.

Later on in this chapter we will return to the problem of the sticker on the bag of apples that was introduced in Chapter 1.

Try to understand the students' reasoning

The most important aspect is perhaps the fact that the teacher should want to understand how students think. During this process, the rule that applies to every conversation also applies here: that which you hear is strongly influenced by your expectations. If you think that you know what the other person is going to say, then you fill in their thoughts. As a result, what the other person is actually thinking may sometimes remain hidden. This can be avoided by asking follow-up questions. Once the students become accustomed to this method, they will become better and better at answering such follow-up questions.

The teacher must radiate the feeling that it is important to truly understand what someone is contributing and that not only the teacher, but also everyone in the class, must be able to follow the reasoning. It is only when such a classroom culture is in place that the children will become interested in the reasoning of other students and will want to compare this with their own ideas. Children are extremely perceptive about whether their teacher is truly interested in what they are thinking or is simply waiting for a specific solution.

Do not avoid complex problems

The curriculum involving fractions, percentages, decimals and proportions is difficult. Therefore, there is a great temptation to keep the problems limited and easy to oversee. For example, teachers think they should not present any problems with fractions and percentages together, they should make sure that the ratio table is available when it is needed, and they should review what the students know about percentages before they continue. Such an approach appears logical, but as a result we shift the task to practicing mathematics rules instead of challenging the students to think about the situation.

Discussion is only useful if the problems that we present to the students are not trivial. The teacher must therefore not avoid difficult questions or hard assignments. A teacher who gives students the space to conceive of solutions themselves will often be astonished by how far they get. For the slower students, they must also be regularly challenged with difficult questions. Perhaps we should say: it is precisely the slower students who must be challenged with such questions, because the smarter children are already asking themselves more difficult questions. The core lessons that we have developed in our project provide examples of mathematics problems that are not easy, but they do offer students sufficiently firm ground. One of the assignments from these lessons is described on page 130.

There must be room to try things and think about the result

Before the class discussion begins, students must be given time to hold a discussion for a few minutes in their own small group; they must all have an opportunity to think about the problem first. The teacher can ask a randomly chosen group what they have come up with in their group. Sometimes the lesson proceeds in two steps - the students hold a discussion in their small group and after that there is a class discussion - but a repeated alternation of small group discussion and general class discussion is usually better. This is because we very often see that the first discussion in the small group does not provide many results, even if the small group discussion was preceded by an extensive discussion about the situation. Often the children do not know how they must approach a problem, and they may not even know what kind of problem it actually is. This doesn't matter, because if the teacher sees that the students do not know how to begin, she can return to a general class discussion. Talking about the first attempts usually provides the opportunity to specify a problem to such an extent that the students can get started.

Do not avoid complex problems

The following assignment was really a "tough one" for students in grade 5.

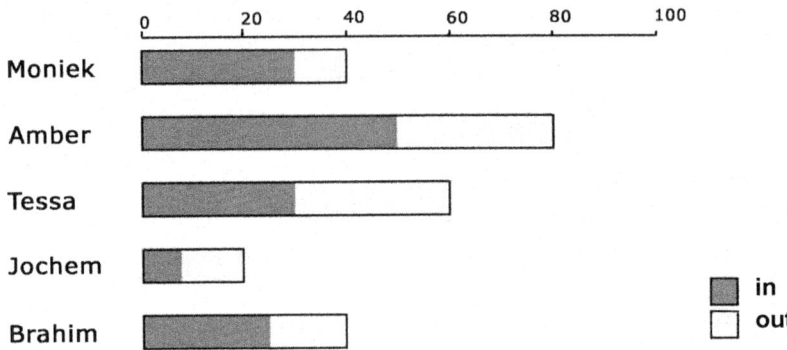

Who can shoot the best with a basketball? Five children practiced shooting baskets this morning. In the graph above you can see how often they scored a basket. However, it is hard to see which one is the best basketball shooter, because the children did not make the same number of throws. Your assignment is to make a list of the children ranging from "best basketball shooter" to "worst basketball shooter".

The problem is difficult because all the bars have different lengths. Moreover, the numbers are not easy ones. The problem can be solved by using either fractions or proportions:

- Using fractions. You can convert the proportion between the number of baskets scored and the number of throws into a fraction. Monique scored with $\frac{3}{4}$ of her throws, Amber $\frac{3}{8}$, Tessa $\frac{1}{2}$, Jochem less than $\frac{1}{2}$ and Brahim $\frac{2}{3}$.
- Using proportions. You can use the following reasoning: "Assume that everyone made an equal number of throws." In this way you make the performances of the various players comparable.

It is precisely because this is such a difficult problem that the assignment offers the possibility to address fundamental issues.

- It concerns proportions. The coloured piece representing "baskets scored" on Amber's bar is larger than that on Monique's, but is Amber actually a better shooter?
- Fractions are a way to convert absolute numbers into a relative standard.
- You can convert performances to a standard to compare them by reasoning: "Assume that...".

Keep the big picture in view

Offering mathematics problems in an open fashion means that the guidance of the teacher becomes crucial. After all, an open discussion can go in various directions, and things often come up in the discussion that are interesting but distract the class from the actual lesson topic. It therefore regularly happens that the teacher will have to terminate certain discussions by shifting the question to something else. If a student brings up a point that is important, but which is not compatible with the discussion at that moment, it is a good idea to write down that point on a corner of the blackboard as something to return to later on. For that matter, the big picture must also be clear to the students. The teacher must ensure that all the students always understand what the central problem is, and she should preferably end the discussion by summarizing what the class has discovered.

Provide new opportunities: return frequently to fundamental issues

Even if the lesson is proceeding very smoothly, it is an illusion to think that the main point addressed in the lesson has been finished once and for all. It is not only the slower students who have a need for things to be repeated. In mathematics education it is actually very easy to build in repetition without having the students become bored; the discussion can be conducted again and again based on a new context problem. If we present students with a problem that is comparable with the previous assignment, perhaps a week or a month after a successful lesson, then in the eyes of the students this is an entirely new problem. At most they will discover during the course of the lesson that "say, this is just like the problem we did when...", but they tend to experience this as a discovery rather than a disappointment.

Establish relationships with previous lessons

It is useful to give names to discoveries that have been made during the school year. For example, during the lesson on decimals (see Chapter 6), Tarik came up with a suggestion to use the odometer of a tractor to measure the size of a piece of land. Since then, the teacher has returned to this discovery periodically with remarks such as "think again about Tarik's odometer". Not only is an approach like this stimulating for the children who made the contribution - Tarik, a slower student, always glowed with pride when "his" odometer was mentioned - but it also helps the students to see that the class as a whole is undergoing a learning process.

It's not about this one problem, it's about the mathematics

In realistic mathematics education, children learn to do math by solving problems. At the moment the teacher presents such a problem, the only thing that counts is that one problem and the solution that the students can come up with. However, in the end mathematics education is not about the concrete problems. It concerns the ideas that you develop as a child by seeking solutions or by discussing various approaches. Of course, this is from the perspective of the teacher; we cannot expect children to look at the mathematics lessons in the same way. Nevertheless, in a class that invests a great deal of time into collectively solving problems, the students eventually understand that it is not the mathematics problems that are at the core, but their own learning process. However, this type of shift will be achieved only after a long time. The moments when which children realize that they have made a discovery, i.e. the moments when they realize that they have begun to think differently, are very important. Looking at your own learning process is called reflection, and this reflection is an important factor in the learning that follows.

Differentiation during class discussions

Every child must be able to participate in the class discussions, but in his or her own way. The teacher must take account of the differences between children.

The points that we discussed in the previous section ensure that an open climate is established in which the children feel challenged to think individually about an mathematics problem, instead of waiting for an explanation. In a similar way, guidelines can be formulated for dealing with differences between children.

Every child can participate

Of course, in every class there are children who like to talk and children who are reluctant when it is their turn. In between these extremes, there are many children who want to participate in the discussion, but who "don't really need to". Such differences within a class are logical, and it would be very difficult to have all students speak for the same length of time during a class discussion. The latter also appears to be essentially unnecessary, because participating does not mean that you have to say something during the discussion. Participating means in the first place that you are thinking about the problem being addressed by the class. The most important precondition for this participation is that the children feel that they are part of the group. If that is the case, they will want to participate in the class discussion, even though that sometimes means that they participate primarily by listening.

Occasionally, certain children cannot follow the discussion at all. Due to the enormous differences within an average class in grades 3 through 6, such situations cannot be avoided entirely. In our view, however, this doesn't mean that certain children should not be allowed to participate in the discussion. And of course it is not such a terrible thing if a child occasionally goes into a daydream during a class discussion.

Everyone's contribution should be taken seriously

The teacher can usually value the contributions from various children. For example, she will see a slower student wrestling with a problem and is happy with every step that the child can take. However, classmates are sometimes cruel in their value judgments and laugh about a remark that they think is stupid. The teacher plays a crucial role here. Often she can make it clear that these "stupid" remarks are also based on reasoning that is actually not so stupid after all. Even more important is that she makes sure there is a class culture in which the students are not all striving to be the smartest one. Of course it is important for students to come up with their own solutions, but trying to understand how other students have approached the problem and following their reasoning is at least as important. The atmosphere must not be competitive. Children should not look too much at each other's performance, but primarily at what they themselves have learned from the other children. Someone who is learning to play a musical instrument does not compare himself of herself with a professional musician; it is more stimulating to look at your own progress, at what you can do now that you couldn't do at first.

Take account of the differences between children

Children have their own preferences in their approach to mathematics problems. For example, there are students who like to draw percentage bars on a piece of scrap paper, while other students prefer to write sums. And if there is a choice between using fractions or proportions, it will probably be the same children who usually reach for the ratio table. If the teacher notices such differences, it is a good idea for her to also pay attention to them; in this way she can emphasize that all children can develop their own mathematics methods.

Of course, teachers pay attention to other differences between children. For example, if a child who doesn't speak very much in class comes up with a suggestion, it goes without saying that a teacher will pay more attention to this reaction than that of a child who always participates fully in the discussion.

Even for the better students, mathematics problems are seldom trivial

The are some children who can usually see an approach to a problem right away. These are also the children who sometimes see immediately that there is more than one way to tackle the problem and who may have so much oversight that they understand that an approach using fractions amounts to the same thing as an approach using proportions. Nevertheless, mathematics problems are seldom trivial even for the smarter children. Perhaps the problem itself is not difficult, but explaining your solution to others and verbalizing your arguments is often a big task. Consequently, smarter children will seldom refuse to participate in a class discussion. However, this assumes that the discussion topic concerns a real problem and not simply how you can figure the next sum on a list of similar sums.

For that matter, the smarter children also tend to have ineffective behaviour when tackling problems. We see this, for example, when we present tough problems to the better mathematics students. It turns out that the smarter children are so accustomed to easily doing the assignments without having to think much about them, that many of them do not write anything on their scrap paper about these tough problems, and therefore do not find a solution.

An occasional lesson to support the better students

We believe that open class discussions can stimulate both the slower students and the better mathematics students, but occasionally choosing a special lesson from the viewpoint of the better students is certainly a good idea. With the lesson "laying tiles" from page 136, we have tried to give an example of such a lesson. The aim of this lesson is to have children think about multiplying fractions. In our view, a sum such as $2\frac{1}{2} \times 3\frac{3}{4}$ is not part of the core objectives of mathematics education in primary school, in any case not in this abstract, formal form. Nevertheless, there are some children who can deal with such sums, also at that formal level. The lesson "laying tiles" concerns a very tangible situation - tiling a terrace - so that all students can participate in the lesson, but it can be used especially for the better students to show them how you can multiply fractions with other fractions.

Taking account of the differences between children, when the differences in mathematical understanding and skill are significant in almost every class, is not a simple task. In our view the key lies in presenting mathematics problems in an open fashion. These problems are open not only in the sense that there are various ways of solving the problem, but especially in the sense that the initiative for solving them lies with the students. The teacher must make it very clear that she does not want the students to find the solution that she has in her head, but to think up a solution themselves. If children take the responsibility for solving a problem, they will use their

Especially for the better mathematics students: laying tiles

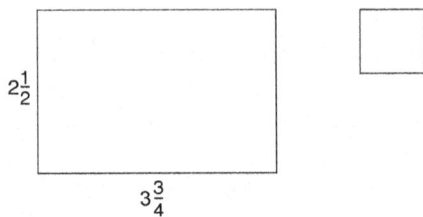

The following problem can enable students to explore multiplication sums such as $2\frac{1}{2} \times 3\frac{3}{4}$. Such multiplication sums are not part of the core objectives of the curriculum, certainly not in this abstract form. Nevertheless, these problems must be addressed because the better students can deal fairly easily with this type of multiplication. We have chosen a problem that is so tangible that all the students can find an answer at a certain level, but the better students will perhaps make the step to more formal reasoning.

A homeowner wants to buy enough large garden tiles for a terrace. Unfortunately, the tiles do not fit neatly onto the place that she has chosen, because they fit $2\frac{1}{2}$ times in one direction and $3\frac{3}{4}$ times in the other direction. How many tiles does she need?

— Every child will probably be able to see that in any case 12 whole tiles would be enough, if you buy 3 × 4 tiles, you can cut a piece off all the edges.
— Children might also come up with the idea that you could still do something with the pieces you cut off. By means of drawing or reasoning, they could come to the conclusion that you could also complete the tiling job with 10 whole tiles.
— This can lead to the children also wanting to know the exact result: it is obviously a number between 9 and 10, but what is it exactly? For the practical situation this does not matter, because if you go to a garden centre you can only buy whole tiles anyway, but if 3 × 4 has an exact result, then $2\frac{1}{2} \times 3\frac{3}{4}$ probably has an exact answer as well. It ultimately amounts to the question of how big the tile is that is placed in the upper right corner of the drawing below, a tile that is $\frac{1}{2} \times \frac{3}{4}$ of a whole tile.
— The size of the tile can then be determined by dividing it into small pieces. This can be the step to taking a routine approach: $2\frac{1}{2} \times 3\frac{3}{4} = 5 \times \frac{1}{2} \times 15 \times \frac{1}{4} = 5 \times 15\,\frac{1}{2} \times \frac{1}{4}$.

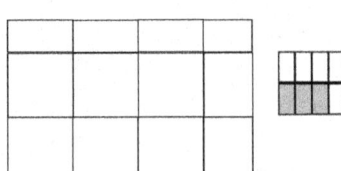

own knowledge instead of waiting for instructions about a suitable approach. And even if the differences in knowledge are great, every child can at least find one part of the solution.

However, it is not easy to give the initiative to the students. Teachers usually feel much more at home in the role of the explainer, in the role of the expert who knows how things are supposed to be and who finds ways to make things clear. When students have a great deal to contribute, it is not really possible to plan how the lesson will proceed, even if the teacher tries beforehand to determine where the children will go. Moreover, a precondition is that the teacher has a sufficient overview of the curriculum and is confident that she will always be able to steer the discussion back to the lesson topic, regardless of where it goes in the meantime.

In this approach, children are also asked to do different things. Instead of being able to wait for an explanation, they are expected to search for solutions themselves and discuss the problem with other students. For that matter, this would be a major change in many classrooms and not one that could be realized from one day to the next.

Differentiation according to precision

Allow students to make estimates and to calculate by rounding off. The better mathematics students will then find the exact answer.

In this section, we want to pay special attention to one specific form of differentiation. When we think of mathematics problems, we usually think of problem situations that are formulated in such an open fashion that various solution methods are possible, but where there is still only a single answer. However, we can also present the task differently in an open fashion by accepting variation in the answers.

The sticker on the sack of apples from Chapter 1 is an example of a problem that we can offer to the students in such an open fashion. The question is not: "exactly how much do you have to pay for this sack of apples?" But: "about how much does this sack of apples cost?" Students can search for an answer in their own way and according to their knowledge of mathematics, so their answers will vary in precision.

The important thing here is not how far away their result is from the exact answer, but the argumentation they use to support their estimate.

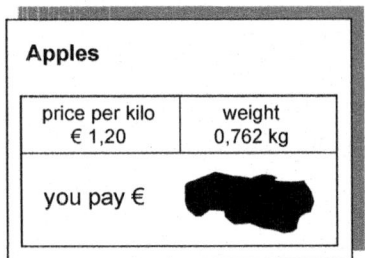

The price sticker on a sack of apples shows the weight of the apples and the price per kilo. However, a blob of ink obscures the actual price. Approximately how much would you have to pay for the sack of apples?

The focus of such a problem is not the answer, but how the children explain their answers: "it must be less than € 1.20, because...", "it is approximately $\frac{3}{4}$ of € 1.20, because...", "100 g costs € 0.12, therefore ...".

By providing the problems in an open fashion, we make room for differentiation in a very natural way. Slower students will perhaps not get any further than a rough estimate, while other students will find the exact answer. For that matter, these approaches can often overlap: students begin with an estimate and during this process discover methods to refine the answer.

Another example with which we can illustrate the idea of differentiation according to precision is the following:

> When you buy something, you pay VAT (sales tax). For many years the VAT rate was $17\frac{1}{2}$ percent. Therefore if the television costs € 400.00 before tax, then the tax of $17\frac{1}{2}$ percent would be added to that € 400.00. How much would you then have to pay for the television?

Can we require that all children are able to work out such a problem at the end of primary school? This specific problem requires formal calculation with rather difficult numbers. But what can we realistically require from children?

We could decide that the mathematics problems should be limited to sums with round percentages such as 20%, 25% and 50%. Such percentages occur relatively often in daily life - during sales for example - and they are very important in estimation and flexible calculation. However, if we only provide problems with round percentages, we would miss the whole point of the percentage concept; if we only had to use such round percentages, the concept of percentage would never have been invented in the first place. If all the percentages were round numbers, simple fractions such as $\frac{1}{5}$ and $\frac{1}{4}$ would have been enough for society.

The second argument is that we should not simplify all percentage problems to sums with round percentages because in doing so we do not prepare children for the world outside school. If faced with a percentage such as $17\frac{1}{2}$ percent, children shouldn't be baffled. Finally, a third argument is that we fail to challenge the better mathematics students with the simplified approach. There are plenty of students who can make the step to formal calculation rules without difficulty. For them, $17\frac{1}{2}$ percent has just as much meaning as 23% or 25%.

The alternative is not to avoid difficult percentages, but to ask students to make a well-founded estimate - similar to multiplying decimals.

About how much is $17\frac{1}{2}$ % of € 400.00?

Possible answers of the students could be the following:

- It is nearly 20%, so about $\frac{1}{5}$; 400 : 5 = 80, therefore the result is approximately € 80.00.
- 10% of € 400.00 is € 40.00; 5% of € 400.00 is half of this, which is € 20.00. 15% of € 400.00 is therefore € 60.00. It is slightly more than € 60.00.

We believe that such answers are more than adequate. Moreover, they demonstrate that the students have insight into the relationships between percentages and fractions.

Of course, there are also ways to find the exact result:

- 10% of € 400.00 is € 40.00; $7\frac{1}{2}$ % is $\frac{3}{4}$ of 10%, therefore you add another € 30.00;
- 1% of € 400.00 is € 4.00; $17\frac{1}{2}$ % is therefore $17\frac{1}{2}$ times € 4.00.

The latter approach uses the 1% rule. It can be applied to every percentage problem, and from our viewpoint as adults seems so self-evident that we tend to teach all students this rule. However, we suggest that teachers delay working with the 1% rule until the students develop a strong network of numerical relationships.

Differentiation according to precision is not a panacea which causes all differentiation problems to disappear. It is compatible with the more general approach to the differentiation issue that we recommend. This approach essentially amounts to giving students a great deal of room to search for their

Slower students can also contribute

During the past two years, Helga and Maaike earned low scores on the national test. They both still have difficulty with sums such as 18 - 12, which is material from grade 2. They do not enjoy mathematics. The teacher in grade 5 has given them extra attention and helps them with specially selected assignments, but Helga and Maaike are otherwise largely keeping pace with the grade 5 programme. In this text box, we have presented several episodes from that year, as described by the teacher, Lia Oosterwaal.

To introduce decimals, I had two lessons where the students measured with bars that were too big (see Chapter 3). The task in the first lesson was: if you have to measure a table with a long bar, how would you subdivide that bar? The task in the second lesson was: if you had a bar that was ten times shorter, but you had to measure your eraser, how would you subdivide that shorter bar? Maaike paid attention during these lessons, but did not really participate in the discussions.

In the third lesson, I presented problems such as: can you write 60 cm as the "so-much part" of a 1 metre bar? And can you also do this for 25 cm?

The 60 cm length was $\frac{6}{10}$ of the long bar, everyone agreed with this. The 25 cm length question resulted in a discussion. Robin said that it is "$\frac{2}{10}$ and a half". Tisse said: "$\frac{2}{10}$ and one-half 10th". Maaike said, "yes, but you don't write it that way", and somewhat later, "it is $\frac{2}{10}$ and then $\frac{1}{5}$". I showed Maaike how much $\frac{1}{5}$ of the bar is.

Other students ultimately came up with a more exact answer: 25 cm is 25 of the little pieces of $\frac{1}{100}$, therefore it is $\frac{25}{100}$. And 60 cm is $\frac{6}{10}$ of 1 metre, but also $\frac{60}{100}$. I drew the longer bar of 1 metre, the short bar of $\frac{1}{10}$ meter and the piece of 1 cm that is $\frac{1}{10}$ of the shorter bar. Everyone appeared to understand, even Maaike, so those two long lessons had a purpose after all. I then had them do a few more problems.

Later on, at the beginning of the gym lesson, Maaike came up to me beaming with happiness: "I get it. Now I can do math, I understand it for the first time."

I had a similar experience with Helga. During the first group lessons, Helga was not really keeping up with the work and she regularly complained about how she didn't have a nice group. Today she had a sour expression; the children were forming new groups for mathematics, and she wasn't happy about this. However, I saw her perk up when I handed out colour copies with a picture of a decoration for the Christmas tree. The balls were coloured in a repeated pattern of green-red-green-red-green-blue, but the children had not yet seen that this was the pattern.

I asked the class which balls were blue. This is an easy one, because you see this immediately: number six number 12 and so on. So they could just use the table of six. More difficult was the question of whether they could predict the location of the green balls. Suddenly, Helga responded: "You can see that the green ball is always next to the blue one and if the blue one is number six, than the green ball will always have to be number five."

At that instant, a light went on for other children as well. They discovered the pattern, by reasoning with the pattern of the striking blue ball that Helga discovered.

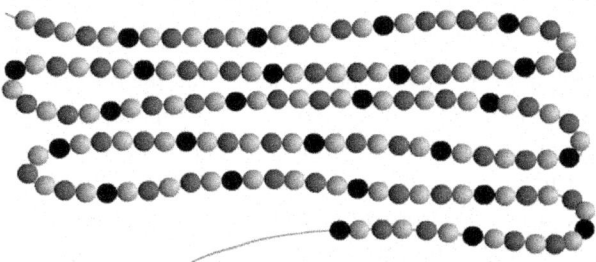

During the break, Helga was still glowing with pride. She had given the class the idea of using the striking blue ball to determine the pattern, and she explained that this step was needed for the solution. She could do math! Later on, I noticed that Helga was starting to enjoy the mathematics lessons. She is taking part more and more frequently.

Of course, a light also went on with me; colours are very important for Helga, therefore I should give more attention to this aspect. For example, on the blackboard I started using coloured chalk more frequently.

Around Easter, we began filling bags with chocolate eggs. I asked the children to decide for themselves the percentage of white chocolate, dark chocolate and milk chocolate eggs in each bag. They could also determine the number of eggs per bag themselves. It was satisfying to see how slower students such as Helga and Maaike could also take part in this activity. Helga: "We are putting 20 eggs into a bag. 50% of them are milk chocolate, which is 10 eggs. So 10 eggs are left over. We want to have 10% dark chocolate eggs; so there were two dark chocolate eggs. Now there are eight eggs remaining, and those are white chocolate. There are 40% white eggs because 50 -10 is 40."

own solutions and stimulating them to get as far as possible on their own power.

Differentiation during individual practice

Not all students cover the same subject matter in the curriculum. During individual practice sessions, give the better students and the gifted children more challenging tasks. Be critical about the problems that you assign. Choose problems that are compatible with what the children understand.

In this chapter we have gone primarily into the role of class discussions and differentiation, because it is specifically this aspect that is experienced as problematic and because some models of class organization essentially amount to avoiding general class discussions. With respect to individual practice, there is probably more agreement. The idea that it is better to present students with different material when they are working individually is probably endorsed by most teachers, although that does not mean that this is easy to organize.

All mathematics textbooks for primary school offer possibilities for differentiation by providing extra pages with review problems and more advanced material. Our impression is that teachers can work well with these additional materials, but that these pages offer insufficient assistance for the two extremes with which every teacher is faced: the slower students and the gifted ones.

The slower students

The concern for slower mathematics students has two important elements: offering them extra help and reflecting critically on the problems that we assign to them. Even if the slower students can participate in the class discussions, this does not mean that they benefit from them in the same way as the rest of the class. Slower students need extra help from the teacher, and this help can be given by forming of a group of students that have difficulty with the curriculum. While the teacher is working with this group, the other students can, for example, work individually on their own assignments. In such a support group, the teacher can review a previous class discussion and determine what the students actually learned. It is often useful to present a comparable problem once again to the students.

The second element that we referred to above is at least as important. In the current mathematics textbooks for primary school, a great deal of space is given to practicing relatively abstract calculation procedures, such as the addition and multiplication of fractions, converting percentages to fractions and decimals and calculating with decimals.

With topics like these, the slower students may perhaps be able to deal with such assignments, but only if the assigned task is placed within a clear context. In the mathematics textbooks, the link to a context situation often remains limited to an occasional illustration above a list of sums. This may be sufficient to give meaning to the sums that follow for some of the students, but this does not apply to the slower students.

Another point that should be taken into account during the choice of assignments is that children must gradually build a network of numerical relationships. In this book, for example, we argue in various chapters that children must first become competent using simple fractions such as $\frac{1}{2}$, $\frac{1}{3}$ and $\frac{1}{4}$ before we give them sums using other fractions. This applies especially to individual practice. It is a good idea to have slower students practice primarily with simple fractions, because these simple fractions also have a meaning for them.

It is therefore important to look very critically at the problems that we assign to slower students. Becoming well versed using a calculation procedure is not very useful if the procedure does not have any meaning for the child, and it would be erroneous to think that understanding arises from practice. It is therefore necessary to choose problems that are compatible with what the students understand. It is especially with the slower students that we must focus on the core concepts of fractions, proportions, percentages and decimals, and the formal calculation procedures are not part of the core concepts.

Gifted children

The Netherlands Institute for Curriculum Development (SLO) publishes a package titled "Compacting and enriching the mathematics lesson" that is especially intended for working with better students and gifted children.[1] The authors argue in favour of having gifted students participate normally in the class discussions, but to modify the material that they work on individually. Practice material and review exercises can largely be eliminated for such students, and the other assignments should be given a more open and challenging character. The authors have developed a complete programme for gifted students to go along with the four most widely used mathematics textbook series in the Netherlands. These programmes have been worked out as "route maps". In this way, the students see what they should do and what they should skip in every lesson. This links up with what we have stated in this chapter concerning mathematics education as a whole: there must be less emphasis on practicing and more emphasis on understanding.

Class discussions are a central element in education, and the assignments that we give to students could be more open and more challenging. Of course, the practical application is not the same for all students. For gifted children the practice material can be eliminated because they have already mastered this part of the curriculum, while for average students and slower students, this material should be limited because they learn little by simply practicing sums. We believe that most students should not necessarily practice less, but practice differently.

The better students and the gifted children must be given different, more challenging tasks when they are working individually. For some of them, these can be problems from their own textbooks, and for others the teacher must use material that has been developed especially for gifted children. At the same time, however, the teacher must ensure that the students do not skip crucial steps during the course of instruction. The "compacting programmes" of the SLO can offer support when selecting the material for the better students.

Conclusion

With fractions, proportions, percentages and decimals, the problem of differentiation is probably even more severe than during other parts of mathematics education. This concerns a part of the curriculum where insight is the most important aspect, and this means that practicing industriously will not make the gap between the slower students in the better ones any smaller. For that matter, shifting the emphasis to class discussions does not make this gap any smaller either; it is quite possible that the better students will make more progress with such an approach than the slower students. In a certain sense, however, the slower students still benefit the most, because learning mathematics changes from the tedious repetition of poorly understood procedures into a process of discovering how things really are.

Much of the present chapter comprised a sketch of the type of interactive education - with active student involvement - that we envision. We have provided this sketch in the form of concrete guidelines for teachers, but we fully realize that the transition that is necessary cannot be made based only on a description on paper. Such a transition - because that is what it is - requires great efforts from everyone who is involved in education: teachers, students at the teachers' colleges, school counsellors, and the developers and authors of school books.

note

1   Janson, Dolf & Anneke Noteboom (2004). *Compacten en verrijken van de rekenles voor (hoog)begaafde leerlingen in het basisonderwijs.* (Compacting and enrichment for gifted students in primary education). Enschede: SLO.

8 Final and intermediate attainment targets

Introduction

In the Netherlands, the subjects of fractions, decimals and percentages are addressed scarcely or not at all before grade 4. The same applies to the more formal side of calculating with proportions. Some of these topics are first addressed only in grade 5. On the other side of the timescale, the national achievement test at the end of primary school is taken at the time when no new subject matter is being introduced - except as material for the faster students. The short time span during which the subjects of fractions, percentages, decimals and proportions are offered leaves little room for distinguishing between intermediate attainment targets that are linked to a specific school year. The description of these targets in this book therefore deviates from those in previous TAL publications.

Moreover, the nature of the curriculum and the differentiation structure that is chosen to go along with this curriculum lead to more emphasis on individual growth than on collective final targets. Another essential characteristic of this curriculum is, in the end, its coherence. This of course has consequences for the description of the attainment targets. An integral target description is compatible with a coherent approach: the targets are therefore not included in the running text, but have been combined in this chapter. Within this integrated target description, we will indicate for each target or intermediate target when it should be achieved.

General aspects

Understanding, numerical relationships, reasoning and procedures

When working on assigned problems in the areas of fractions, percentages, decimals and proportions, students can use the network of numerical relationships that they have developed over the years. For example, they know that $\frac{3}{4}$ is the same as $\frac{1}{2} + \frac{1}{4}$ and they can use that knowledge with problems such as $\frac{3}{4} + \frac{3}{4} = $. We are referring here to using numerical relationships which the student comes up with directly when there is occasion for this. The actual utilization of this knowledge is then only a small additional step. However, students also encounter situations for which their knowledge of numerical relationships is insufficient. In that case, they often can still find an answer by means of reasoning, by using their insight into meaning and relationships. During this reasoning, they of course fall back on the same knowledge, but in this case it is deployed in an activity that has much more the character of problem solving. In this situation, the student will need more time to arrive at a solution.

Finally, there are also students who have meanwhile developed routines or standard procedures which they can use insightfully.

In this chapter we will develop our previous statements about core insights into a series of targets. When distinguishing between these targets, we will follow the distinction that we made above concerning the use of numerical relationships, reasoning and using *standard procedures*. However, we will begin with a number of targets that should be directly linked to *insight*. Insight forms the basis of everything. It is given its own place because it concerns a general quality which permeates all activities.

The mastery of standard calculation procedures is not a target for all students. Due to the risk of "trick-like" routine, teachers should be reserved on this point. Instead, we prefer to emphasize the insightful use of the *calculator* in addition to estimation and skilful calculation. However, procedures can become differential targets for some of the students.

We will discuss the targets under the following headings:
- insight into meaning and relationship;
- knowledge and use of numerical relationships;
- reasoning;
- insightful use of the calculator;
- using procedures (differential target).

Where necessary, we will provide the targets with an explanation and examples.

Insight into meaning and relationship

The curriculum is characterized by the strong relationship between fractions, percentages, decimals and proportions. This relationship emerges from the fact that they are essentially all variations on the same theme: proportions. With fractions, percentages, decimals and proportions, the underlying relationship is not described with multiple numbers, but with only a single number. Like Freudenthal[1], we refer here to measuring or proportion numbers.

Besides acquiring insight into this relationship, the student must also understand the differences between fractions, percentages, decimals and proportions. These are differences that have to do with the reason why these concepts emerged, their meaning and how they are used in practice. Fractions describe proportions as part-whole relationships. With decimals, the measurement aspect comes to the foreground. In context situations they are usually linked to units. Percentages make it easier to calculate and compare by reducing proportions to standard ratios: some amount to 100.

Taken together, this leads to the following targets.

Insight into the relationship between fractions, percentages, decimals and proportions

The student is aware of the kinship between fractions, percentages, decimals and proportions and understands the relationships between the various description forms. (At the end of grade 5).

Fractions, percentages, decimals and proportions as measuring or proportion numbers

The student understands that fractions, proportions, decimals and percentages in context problems always concern measuring or proportion numbers and always realizes what the unit is to which the fraction, proportion, decimal or percentage refers.

This also means that the student associates fractions, decimals and percentages primarily with part-whole relationships and not so much with procedures such as: "$\frac{3}{4}$ means dividing into four pieces and taking three of those pieces" or: "15% is dividing by 100 and multiplying by 15". (Halfway through grade 5).

Decimals as systematic refinement

The student can interpret the sequence of numbers in a decimal as a series of "common decimal fractions" with denominators having increasing powers of 10; the student also realizes that these correspond with systematically refined units or measurement units. (At the end of grade 5).

Percentages as a standardization via "hundredths" or "so much to 100"

The student understands that descriptions with percentages form an alternative for descriptions with fractions or proportions and understands the advantages and disadvantages of this standardized description method. (At the end of grade 5).

Proportions as proportional and absolute reasoning

The student realizes that you can compare numbers or units in context situations proportionally or in absolute terms, and can use both approaches in a sensible fashion. The student is aware that proportional comparison is sometimes also used in situations where we "pretend" that there is direct proportionality. (At the end of grade 5).

Explanation
For example, when a comparison is made between the criminality in two cities, then we often reason as if there was a direct linear proportion, i.e. we pretend that the number of cases of criminality is directly proportional to the number of residents of the city.

Numerical relationships

In the section above we described insight into the relationship between the various sub-areas as one of the main themes for the curriculum. This relationship also emerges in the following:

– Knowing and using numerical relationships within and between the sub-areas.
– Using numerical relationships and insights for flexible calculation and estimation.

There is overlap between these two components, but for the purposes of clarity we will describe them below as separate from each other.

Knowing and using numerical relationships

The student can deal flexibly with simple numerical relationships between fractions, percentages, decimals and proportions. (Within the sub-areas at the end of grade 5; between the sub-areas at the end of grade 6.)

Explanation
We use the term numerical relationships to refer not only to relationships within a sub-area but also relationships between fractions, percentages, decimals and proportions. When calculating, students must be able to make the transition from one type of fraction to another, or from one proportion to another, but also from proportions to fractions, from fractions to percentages, and so forth. These attainment targets concern simple fractions - fractions with denominators of 2, 3, 4, 5, 8, 10, 100 and 1000 - and the corresponding proportions, decimals and percentages.

Regarding percentages, this means that the student has access to reference points for evaluating the order of magnitude of percentages. This also concerns multiples of 10%, 25% and $33\frac{1}{3}$% using the association with the corresponding fractions. The knowledge of multiples of $12\frac{1}{2}$% can also be used as a possible expansion for some students. This concerns primarily percentages above 100, such as 150% is $1\frac{1}{2}$ times as much and 200% is two times as much.

Examples
Numerical relationships within a sub-area:

-   The student knows the fraction $\frac{3}{4}$ as $\frac{1}{2}+\frac{1}{4}$, as $3\times\frac{1}{4}$ and as $1-\frac{1}{4}$, and can use this knowledge when solving a problem such as $\frac{3}{4}+\frac{3}{4}=$ by thinking that $\frac{3}{4}+\frac{3}{4}=\frac{1}{2}+\frac{1}{4}+\frac{1}{2}+\frac{1}{4}=1+\frac{1}{2}$. Or by interpreting $\frac{3}{4}+\frac{3}{4}$ as $1-\frac{1}{4}+\frac{1}{4}+\frac{1}{2}=1\frac{1}{2}$, or by seeing $\frac{3}{4}+\frac{3}{4}$ as $3\times\frac{1}{4}+3\times\frac{1}{4}=6\times\frac{1}{4}=1\frac{1}{2}$.
-   The student associates 0.25 with $4\times0.25=1$ and with $3\times0.25=0.75$.
-   The student is familiar with relationships such as $10\times0.1=1$; $10\times0.01=0.1$ and $0.1\times0.1=0.01$.

– The student knows multiples of 25%, such as $2 \times 25\% = 50\%$, $3 \times 25\% = 75\%$, $4 \times 25\% = 100\%$, $5 \times 25\% = 125\%$.

Numerical relationships between fractions, proportions, decimals and percentages:

– The student associates 31% with "approximately $\frac{3}{10}$" or "slightly less than $\frac{1}{3}$".
– The student recognizes a proportion such as 24 : 36 as 2 : 3.
– A proportion such as 80 to 320 - for example in the context of 80 g of sugar to 320 g of candy - is interpreted by the student as a part-whole relationship that can be visualized with a bar and can be simplified to 1 to (or 1 of) 4. The student realizes that this corresponds with $\frac{1}{4}$, which is associated with 0.25, or $\frac{25}{100}$ and 25%. The student can then link this back to other sub-areas by utilizing the knowledge that 25% corresponds with 25 to 100, which is equal to 1 to 4 and to 80 of 320, and the student knows that this can be checked by calculating 80 : 320 = 0.25 on the calculator.
– The student can solve a problem such as: "how much do 0.750 kg of apples cost at € 3.80 per kilo?". By converting this into $\frac{3}{4}$ of € 3.80, which can in turn be split into $\frac{1}{2}$ of € 3.80 and $\frac{1}{4}$ of € 3.80 and results in € 1.90 + € 0.95 = € 2.85.
– The student can solve this problem by understanding 0.750 as $\frac{750}{1000}$ and conducting the calculation as 3.80 : 1000 = 0.0038 and 750 × 0.0038 = 2.8500. Or by thinking that 2 × 0.750 = 1.5 and first calculating the price of 1.5 kg; 1.5 kg costs € 3.80 + € 1.90 = € 5.70 and € 5.70 divided by 2 is € 2.85.

Using numerical relationships for estimation

The student is capable of modifying the numbers in problems (including context problems) involving fractions, percentages, decimals and proportions in such a way that he can obtain a global answer using a simple calculation with "easy numbers". (This applies for all school years and for the levels corresponding to those school years - i.e. corresponding to the numerical relationships that the students have mastered at that time. This target is not fully achieved until the end of grade 6.)

Explanation
This does not concern the application of a standard procedure for rounding off, but the simplification of the calculation by choosing "easy" numbers with which you can calculate easily. The definition of "easy" numbers depends in turn on the numerical relationships described above and the degree with which the student understands these relationships. With approximation or estimation, differentiation in precision is possible, where it is important that the student understands the extent to which the precision of the result is compatible with the situation.

Examples
–   In a problem such as "how much does 0.762 kg of apples cost at a price of € 3.80 per kilo?", the student recognizes 0.762 as approximately 0.750 or 0.75. Or the student realizes that the $\frac{762}{1000}$ (or 762 of 1000) corresponds with approximately $\frac{3}{4}$.
–   The student brings the given percentages into connection with "easy" percentages such as 25% and $33\frac{1}{3}$%, but can also relate these to the nearest multiple of 10. For example, this took place when interpreting the results of a vote where 60% were in favour; the student determined that there was a majority in favour (more than half), but that this was not a $\frac{2}{3}$ majority.

Reasoning

Reasoning about operations with fractions

The student can conduct reasoned operations with fractions in simple situations. (At the end of grade 6. Repeated addition and subtraction at the end of grade 5.)

Explanation
This primarily involves finding the sum and the difference. Using reasoning to determine a product or quotient remains limited to cases in which a fraction and a whole number are combined. The aim here is not to understand and apply standard procedures; when the student uses a rule, he must be able to explain this rule in terms of the concrete situation.

Examples
-   With a problem such as $\frac{1}{2} + \frac{1}{3} =$, the student can explain how you can make sixths from halves and thirds, up to the level of an explanation such as "a denominator that is twice as big means that two times as many pieces go into a whole and that the pieces are therefore twice as small, or half as big."
-   The student realizes that a problem such as $12 \times 1\frac{1}{2} =$ can be solved with repeated addition.
-   The student can convert a problem such as $2\frac{1}{2} \times 12$ into "two times 12 plus half of 12" (see reasoned multiplication).
-   The student can explain that a problem such as $\frac{3}{4} : 2 =$ can be solved by dividing all the "pieces" into two and by reasoning that in this way you arrive at $\frac{3}{8}$.
-   The student realizes that you can convert dividing by a fraction into the repeated subtraction of that fraction from that number or by determining the proportion between the number and the fraction.

The examples are described as non-context sums here, but what is especially important is that the students should be able to deal with such problems when they are offered in a context form. However, the better students are expected to perform these types of reasoning without a context.

Reasoned operations with decimals

The student can use his knowledge and insight into the structure and meaning of decimals when performing operations with decimals, and in usual situations can make skilful use of shifting measurement scales, to both eliminate decimals and to reason about the relationships between fractions and decimals. (At the end of grade 6.)

Explanation
The possibility of the operation is determined by the question of whether there is only one decimal involved or more than one. For dividing a whole number by a decimal and for multiplying a decimal by a whole number, the student can use column calculation[2]. The basis for this method lies in repeated subtraction or repeated addition. For multiplication of a decimal by another decimal and for writing the remainder as decimals to the right of the decimal point, the student can shift measurement scales.

Final and intermediate attainment targets

Examples

Using the relationship with simple decimal fractions:

—   The student can calculate the result of 2.195 + 1.9 = or 2.195 - 1.9 = by converting 2.195 into $\frac{2195}{1000}$ and 0.9 into $\frac{9}{10} = \frac{900}{1000}$, or to realize that with these relationships in mind the problem corresponds with 2.195 + 1.900 = and 2.195 - 1.900 = .

—   The student solves a problem such as 24 × 3.47 = for example by means of repeated addition and a problem such as 269 : 25.8 = by means of repeated subtraction.

Here as well, the problems are given without any context, but the important thing is that the students can deal with such problems when they are offered in context form.

Switching measurement scales:

—   The student can solve problems such as the sums listed above 24 × 3.47 = and 269 : 25.8 = by switching measurement scales, for example by replacing € 3.47 in a context problem with 347 cents. (Some students can also do this at a more formal level by temporarily replacing 24 × 3.47 with 24 × 347 and then dividing the result by 100.)

—   The student can solve a problem such as € 2.89 + € 3.65 = by first adding up the cents and then the whole euros together, or by first converting everything into cents.

—   The student can convert $\frac{1}{4}$ litre into 0.250 litre by thinking that one litre corresponds with 1000 ml and that $\frac{1}{4}$ litre is therefore equivalent to 250 ml.

—   The student can provide an answer or make an estimate for a problem such as "how much do 1.8 kg of apples cost at € 1.20 per kilo?" by switching between kilograms and grams and between euros and cents.

Reasoning with percentages

The student can use knowledge and insight into the structure and meaning of percentages when calculating and figuring with percentages; in the usual cases, the student makes skilful use, if necessary, of the double bar, number line or ratio table in order to modify the proportion numbers in a step-by-step fashion. (At the end of grade 6.)

Explanation

We can make a distinction between situations in which the percentage must be calculated ("what percent is 130 of 520?"), the part ("how much is 25% of 520?"), or the whole ("how much is 100% if 25% is 130?"). For that matter, it is not our intention to distinguish these three situations as unrelated "cases" that the students must know as such. A combination of numerical knowledge and insight must be sufficient to arrive at a reasoned answer in all cases. At the same time, a distinction can be made between the skilful use of numerical relationships and more general approaches that are independent of the numbers in the problem.

The skilful use of numerical relationships concerns approaches where the student modifies proportion numbers in a step-by-step fashion. (See also "Reasoning with proportions".)

If the numbers do not lend themselves to easy calculation, the student can make the intermediate step of calculating one percent. To find a percentage, for example, the student can first calculate how much 1% of the "whole" is, and then determine how many times this fits into the given "part". In order to take a percentage of the "whole", the student can first calculate how much 1% of the "whole" is and then multiply this with the given percentage. Note that the latter approach in practice amounts to the same thing as converting the percentage into "so many hundredths". This can also be interpreted as a process of first dividing the "whole" by 100 and then multiplying with the percentage.

Examples

—   The student determines how many percent 175 is of the 625 people surveyed by means of a step-by-step modification of the numbers.

number in favour	175	35	7	28
number sur-veyed	625	125	25	100

Or by first calculating 1% of 625 and then dividing 175 by the answer (6.25).

— The student calculates how many grams of pure gold is contained in a chain weighing 396 grams, which is 35% gold, by step-by-step modification of the numbers.

percentage	100%	25%	10%	35%
weight	396	99	39.6	138.6

Or by first calculating 1% of 396 and then multiplying the result (3.96) by 35 (35% is 35 × 3.96 g = 138.6 g).

Reasoning with proportions

With a given pair of proportion numbers, the student can construct a series of equivalent number pairs and can also express the proportion described by these number pairs in a fraction or a percentage. Moreover, the student is familiar with the strategies that can be used to produce equivalent number pairs.

Explanation
This concerns strategies that can be made visible with the ratio table such as doubling, taking halves, addition, taking the difference, and multiplying or dividing by the same number.

Examples
— The student compares the prices of two different packages of the same product, 250 g for € 3.65 and 200 g for € 3.25 by calculating how much a specific quantity (such as 1000 g, 100 g or 50 g) costs in both cases.
— Based on the actual numbers, the student can determine that there are more bicycles in total in France than in the Netherlands, but that the Netherlands has proportionally more bicycles (compared to the number of residents).
— The student can estimate the answer of 14% of € 720.00 by calculating 15% using a ratio table.

percentage	100%	10%	5%	15%
amount	€ 720,00	€ 72,00	€ 36,00	€ 108,00

Conclusion: 14% of € 720.00 is slightly less than € 108.00. When the student realizes that 1% is approximately € 7.00, 14% of € 720.00 can be estimated as approximately € 100.00. If desired, a more precise answer can be obtained by calculating 1%.

percentage	100%	10%	5%	15%	1%	14%
amount	€ 720.00	€ 72.00	€ 36.00	€ 108.00	€ 7.20	€ 100.80

When an exact answer is intended, a more direct method is obvious, either:

percentage	100%	1%	14%
amount	€ 720.00	€ 7.20	€ 100.80

or:

percentage	100%	1400%	14%
amount	€ 720.00	€ 1008.00	€ 100.80

– The student can convert a statement such as "about 500 of the 800 cars being transported on the ship were lost" into a percentage by using the ratio table.

part	500	250	125	62.5
whole	800	400	200	100

By using the ratio table, the student can determine that 500 of 800 is equivalent to 62.5% of the whole, which can be rounded off to slightly more than 60%.

Multiplicative reasoning

The student knows how to convert context-linked descriptions of multiplicative relationships in terms of fractions, decimals and percentages into multiplication problems. (At the end of grade 6.)

Explanation
This is a difficult target which requires more attention to achieve than is usually the case.

Examples
— The student knows that "$\frac{2}{3}$ of" can be written out in calculation form as "$\frac{2}{3} \times$...".
— The student knows that "0.64 grams at... price" can be written out as "0.64 ×...".
— The student knows that "150% of ..." can be written out as "1.50 × ..."
— The student can reason that you can find an unknown percentage by determining the quotient of the part and the whole. For example, by converting the results of a survey into percentages; according to the survey, 358 of 987 people surveyed indicated that they thought airplane noise was a nuisance.
— A possible additional step for some of the students could be the following: the student can reason that a price including 17.5% VAT amounts to 117.5 times the original price.

The calculator

Working with the calculator is a continuation of reasoning with operations. However, strategies for skilful calculation, where the student is led by the specific numbers in the problem, are less suitable for working with the calculator. With respect to finding percentages, this applies especially to strategies where the result is approached in steps. A more general strategy, for example where first 1% is calculated, is much more compatible with using the calculator.

After leaving primary school, a great deal of calculation work will be performed with the calculator. In practice, working out problems by hand or doing mental arithmetic with fractions, percentages, decimals and proportions primarily concerns figuring with simple numbers and making estimations. The more complex calculation work is done on the calculator. In this context, we distinguish the following targets.

Converting fractions into decimals using the calculator

The student understands that you can convert fractions into decimals using the calculator by dividing the numerator by the denominator. (At the end of grade 5.)

Working with decimals on the calculator

The students can complete simple calculations (+, -, × and :) with decimals on the calculator. The students are aware that it is advisable to check the result of the computation on the calculator afterwards by making an estimate. (At the end of grade 5.)

Finding percentages with the calculator

The student can use the calculator insightfully when finding percentages and calculating with percentages. (At the end of grade 6.)

Explanation
This primarily concerns general strategies for reasoning with operations using percentages that are independent of the numbers in the problem. For example, these are strategies that are based on calculating 1%. In this way, the

student can reason as follows:

— you can convert a "part-whole" relationship into a percentage by dividing the "whole" by 100 and then determine how frequently the "part" fits into this;
— you can calculate the "part" by first figuring the value of 1% (by dividing the "whole" by 100) and multiplying this by the percentage;
— you can calculate the "whole" by first figuring the value of 1% and then multiplying this by 100.

Students who have mastered multiplicative reasoning at a formal level will also be able to take a percentage of a "whole" by converting the percentage into a decimal and multiplying the "whole" by this decimal. There are also students who can see that you can convert a part-whole relationship by means of division into a decimal, and that you can in turn convert this into a percentage.

Procedures (differential)

As previously noted, the mastery of procedures is not a target that must be pursued for all students. Moreover, many of the targets that we refer to here correspond with the targets that were formulated for working with the calculator. This also places the importance of mastering procedures within this domain in perspective. However, it must be noted that many mathematical procedures have a cultural value and that the mastery of procedures can make mathematics in secondary education easier.
Of course, different procedures are possible. The following are procedures that are compatible with the intended learning-teaching trajectory.

Routine addition and subtraction of fractions

The student can routinely add and subtract fractions, for example by finding the common denominator, or by choosing a suitable sub-unit of measurement.

Routine multiplication of fractions

The student can multiply fractions in a routine fashion, for example by sep-

arating numerators and denominators. (A multiplication sum such as $\frac{4}{5} \times \frac{2}{3}$ then is converted via $\frac{4}{5} \times \frac{2}{3} = 4 \times \frac{1}{5} \times 2 \times \frac{1}{3}$ into $4 \times 2 \times \frac{1}{15} = \frac{8}{15}$).[2]

Explanation
This is compatible with the model of a tiled terrace, where the original area unit (one tile) is replaced by a smaller one ($\frac{1}{15}$ tile).

Routine division of fractions

The student can routinely solve division problems with fractions, for example by interpreting the division as a proportion so that it can be converted into a division sum without fractions. (A division sum such as $8 \frac{1}{2} : 1 \frac{1}{4}$ is then converted into 34:5 by multiplying the dividend and divisor by four.)

Routine addition and subtraction of decimals

For adding and subtracting decimals, the student can use procedures developed for whole numbers[3] by taking account of the position of the decimal point.

Routine multiplication and division of decimals

For the multiplication and division of decimals, the student can use procedures developed for whole numbers[4] by first leaving out the decimal points and then replacing them.

Routine conversion of proportions

The student can use the ratio table in a routine fashion to convert a number pair into an equivalent number pair, for example by taking one standard interim step.

Example
– The student determines how many percent 175 is of the 625 people surveyed by taking an interim step.

number in favour	175	0,28	28
number surveyed	625	1	100

Making routine calculations with percentages

The student can calculate how much the part is that corresponds with a given percentage of a "whole", for example by first calculating the value of 1% and then multiplying the result with the percentage, or by interpreting the percentage as a factor and using it to multiply the "whole".

Moreover, the student can calculate a percentage when the part and the whole are given, for example by dividing the "part" by the "whole" and multiplying the result by 100, or by first calculating 1% of the "whole" and then dividing that into the "part".

notes

1 Freudenthal, H. (1973). *Mathematics as an Educational Task.* Dordrecht: Reidel.

2 See Van den Heuvel-Panhuizen, M. (Ed.)(2001).*Children Learn Mathematics. A learning-teaching trajectory with intermediate attainment targets for calculation with whole numbers in primary school.* Utrecht: Freudenthal Institute, Utrecht University.

3 See note 2.

4 See note 2.

Lightning Source UK Ltd.
Milton Keynes UK
UKOW04f0622091116

287221UK00008B/249/P